QUILTING MANUAL

Dolores A. Hinson

Drawings by the author

DOVER PUBLICATIONS, INC.
NEW YORK

Published in Canada by General Publishing Company, Ltd.,
30 Lesmill Road, Don Mills, Toronto, Ontario.
Published in the United Kingdom by Constable and Company, Ltd., 10 Orange Street, London WC2H 7EG.

This Dover edition, first published in 1980, is an unabridged
and unaltered republication of the revised and enlarged edition
of *Quilting Manual* originally published in 1970. This edition is
published by special arrangement with Hearthside Press, Inc.,
publishers of the original edition.

International Standard Book Number: 0-486-23924-1
Library of Congress Catalog Card Number: 79-55841

Manufactured in the United States of America
Dover Publications, Inc.
180 Varick Street
New York, N.Y. 10014

A. Author's quilt "Race to the Moon". Blue ribbon winner at the Wood-lawn Needlework Exhibition, Mount Vernon, Virginia, 1968.

B. Author's quilt "The Doll House". Blue ribbon winner at the Woodlawn Needlework Exhibition, Mount Vernon, Virginia, 1970. This child's quilt has two small cloth dolls which can be made to live in the house because each room has a pocket fit into the furniture to hold the dolls. The pocket is below the window in the attic; in the bed in the bedroom; in the chair in the living room; in the car in the garage; and behind the tablecloth in the kitchen.

FOREWORD

The material in this treatise on American quilts is a systematic compilation of data pertinent to the subject and is the product of a number of years devoted to research and investigation. During this period I examined contemporary documents and those prepared more than a century ago. A wealth of information was obtained through personal contacts with quilters, quilt collectors, and curators of museums.

My initial interest in quilts and quilting was stimulated by a conversation with a University of Maryland professor who was also interested in the subject. I developed a hobby of collecting quilt patterns and perusing available books and articles on the various aspects of quilts. It became apparent that although these publications contained excellently prepared material, they also revealed certain voids which precluded a comprehensive coverage.

This book was prepared to present a comprehensive coverage and to inspire interested persons to pursue this fascinating avocation. I cannot recall a hobby as rewarding as a well-made quilt. There are few pastimes that require so little capital investment. The principal materials are interest and stick-to-it-iveness.

Dolores A. Hinson

ACKNOWLEDGEMENT

I gratefully acknowledge the timely suggestions of Mrs. Retha Gambaro made when this book was first outlined. Her interest has lasted to the present time.

Acknowledgements and appreciation are also expressed for the many courtesies accorded me during the time I was doing research on varied aspects of quilts; in particular, for the valued assistance rendered by Mrs. Helen M. Fede of the Mount Vernon Ladies' Association of the Union, Mount Vernon, Virginia; Mrs. J. Elmer Weisheit of the Star Spangled Banner House, Baltimore, Maryland; Mrs. Elsie M. Peters of the Woodrow Wilson Birthplace Foundation, Staunton, Virginia; Mrs. Claire Parker of the James Buchanan Foundation for the Preservation of Wheatland, Lancaster, Pennsylvania; Mr. Russell A. Gibbs of the Washington's Birthplace National Monument, Washington's Birthplace, Virginia; Miss Doris M. Bowman of the Smithsonian Institution, Washington, D.C.; and Mr. Frank J. O'Brien of the Brandywine Battlefield Park Commission, West Chester, Pennsylvania.

The Prince George's County Memorial Library Association has rendered a valuable service in obtaining for me information from books I could not have found otherwise. The unfailing interest, good humor, and helpfulness of the librarians of the Greenbelt branch made this book a much easier and more pleasant task than it could have been.

I wish to thank all the ladies who shared their memories with me and allowed me to see and draw their quilts for this volume.

I wish to thank Mr. and Mrs. Ernest Walker for their help in assembling this book in its final form.

Most of all I wish to thank my mother, Mrs. Iris Codling, for encouragement, help and timely criticism.

Contents

1. *Dainty chintz sprays and wreaths were cut out and appliquéd to the squares of this fine quilt. The work was done so meticulously that it took a mother and daughter forty years to finish. It was started sometime around 1820. (James Buchanan Foundation for the Preservation of Wheatland, Lancaster, Pennsylvania.)*

I

A SHORT HISTORY
OF QUILTS

The lovely designs of American quilts, the highly imaginative names used for patterns, and the documentation of the many famous, and other not so famous, quilts combine to form a little-known section of the American story. Through quilts, we are able to view history from a woman's perspective.

The quilting of cloth came into being when the people who invented weaving reasoned that two or even three thicknesses of cloth would be warmer than one thickness. For centuries the Chinese used quilted cloth to make their characteristically padded winter clothing. The Crusaders found that the quilted shirts worn by the Arabs in the Near East when worn as an undergarment beneath chain mail prevented chafing more effectively than the shirts of single layers of cloth they had always worn.

The European Quilt

These quilted shirts, when brought back to Europe, suggested the bed quilt to European women. The idea spread quite rapidly when a change in the Gulf Stream brought a period of bitter cold winters to western and southern Europe during parts of the thirteenth and fourteenth centuries. The use of warmer clothing and bedding than had been used previously became imperative during these cold periods.

Queens quilted in their palaces and peasant women quilted in their cottages. Some of the many beautiful quilting patterns, described in a later chapter, were developed at this time. Since then, these beautiful patterns have been handed down from one generation to the next (many without substantial changes) to the present day. The ancient patterns were simple ones at first. As women became more expert at this new needlecraft, elaborate patterns were worked out by the seamstresses. As styles changed and became more or less intricate, so the quilting patterns changed to conform. One of these ancient patterns, the Princess' Feather, originally called the Prince's Feather, was copied from the coat of arms of the original Prince of Wales who became Edward II of England in 1307. It was developed in the shires of Northumberland and Durham where variations of the basic pattern were handed down from mother to daughter as family heirlooms. Each family had its own traditional feather form and manner of using it. The Princess' Feather was brought to these shores by the early settlers and has been a favorite pattern ever since for both quilting and appliqué.

European quilts were usually part of matching sets called bed furniture. These sets consisted of quilts, bed curtains, canopies, and what are now called dust ruffles. All of the pieces of the set were made of the same fabric, usually a rich, fine velvet, or at least as expensive and long-wearing a material as the family could afford. They were sometimes embroidered or appliquéd and finally each piece was elaborately quilted. The patchwork quilt, which in the United States is generally thought of as the only kind of quilt, was completely unknown.

Immigration to America

In the year 1620 the English Pilgrims boarded the Mayflower for their journey to the New World. Safely tucked into each person's baggage were his or her personal bedcovers including a generous number of quilts.

Transportation by ship in those early times did not require

that the captain or crew assume the responsibility of providing conveniences and comfort for passengers. It devolved upon the passengers, therefore, to provide for their own personal comfort and necessities, including food. Hard wooden shelves served as beds during the voyage. Bedding and the curtains between the shelf beds for providing a semblance of privacy were furnished by the quilts and blankets from the Pilgrims' luggage. The use of blankets for curtains entailed a sacrifice of some blankets which were so badly needed for their comfort.

The Mayflower's voyage to the New World covered the period from September 6 to November 11, 1620, but the Pilgrims lived on their ship from June 1620 until the following spring when their new homes were completed. From this, it may be supposed that their clothing and bedding were badly worn and sadly in need of replacement even before leaving the ship. They were landed on a wild and barren shore far north of the place they had thought to settle. Even if they had landed in Virginia as planned, the hardships and extremes of temperature to be faced in the New World were underestimated. Songs were sung, and tales were told of flowers in winter, warm weather throughout the year, pearls in the rivers, gold in the ground, gems in the rocks, and the "nut brown maidens" all waiting to be enjoyed by the lucky ones who adventured across the ocean. The sailors and explorers who carried these tales to England were victims of a natural mistake, for they visited Virginia in the summer when the weather was good and the "naturals," as they called the Indians, were harvesting their crops. The naturals ate and otherwise consumed their summer crops each year, saving only enough grain for seed, and then stoically endured the starvation which followed, because they knew no other way of life. The colonists were deceived by these stories and were as misinformed as if the stories had been told maliciously. The colonists also overlooked the fact that their equipment must last a long time since ships from Europe were indefinite in number and their arrival infrequent. The homes and stores they were familiar with in England and Holland were nonexistent in the New World. The

barest necessities had to be found in a raw state and the tools
to wrest them into a usable form were not available. Suitable
tools had to be fashioned to meet the particular requirements.
Their adopted land would have been difficult for experienced
pioneers accustomed to hardships, but the Pilgrims were mostly
city folks. Hard work was familiar to them, it is true, but they
were skilled in one kind of work, performed only to earn their
living. They depended upon the products of others to fill their
household needs. Here they must clear land, build towns, hunt
foods, farm, nurse the sick, make the laws, and do all the other
tasks that go into making a land civilized. This would be a
staggering task for strong, well people. But the Pilgrims were
ill from a long, hard voyage, months of storms at sea, home-
sickness, and inadequate food. They developed scurvy on the
ship, they brought tuberculosis with them from England and
when they landed, a raging epidemic which the Pilgrims simply called "the sickness" struck them down. Here is a quote
from Gilbert Winlow's diary for February 16, 1621:

> "Two months have passed since we sailed in here to New
> Plymouth harbour and the sick set themselves to tame
> the wilderness wastes. And our plain tale is of cold, weari-
> ness, hunger and death. It is the getting wet of cold, poorly
> fed bodies and the going back and forth to the ship to
> sleep in all weathers, that kills us. Twenty-one are dead
> in the two months gone of a sort of galloping consump-
> tion, that when once it gets a grip, tears through the
> scurvy-tainted, half-starved body and carries it off in a
> week or less; which is what we call 'the sickness' . . ."

At times that winter there were only six people able to be
on their feet to tend the others who were more ill than themselves.

When the colony staggered to its feet in the spring, more
than half of the Pilgrims were dead. The rest had to do all the
work that was needed to grow and preserve enough food to
last through the next winter, and to provide what other few
necessities they could manage.

It seems odd to think that out of this experience of misery

could emerge a handicraft that has enriched and brightened our lives ever since, but such is the case.

Clouting or Patching Becomes a Necessity

Old clothing had been patched for reuse ever since people wore clothing, but quilts were used many years before they finally wore out. In the old world, patching the worn-out quilt was not necessary. It was used for rags or stuffing and a new quilt was made from lengths of cloth available either from a shop or loomed by the housewives. But the Pilgrims did not have these lengths of cloth, in fact a poem written in 1630, "The Forefather's Song," included this verse:

"And now our garments begin to grow thin,
And wool is much wanted to card and to spin.
If we can get a garment to cover without,
Our other in-garments are clout upon clout.
Our cloths we brought with us are apt to be torn,
They need to be clouted soon after they're worn,
But clouting our garments they hinder us nothing,
Clouts double are warmer than single whole clothing."

Clouting or, as we would say, patching was used to keep old blankets and quilts in use until cloth could be brought over from England. Even then women would not make their quilts in the old way, because new clothing was a more pressing need than new bedcovers.

The Navigation Acts

To protect her own economy, one of the first things England did following the founding of her colonies was to pass the so-called Navigation Acts. These acts were intended to gather all the colonial shipping and agricultural commodities into English control and allow the colonies to receive goods only in English ships. The colonies then could receive only English goods and were permitted to produce only those articles needed by England. Any products needed by the colonies but produced in competition with English goods were prohibited.

Because of England's great cloth industries, over one-third of her exports was woolen cloth. The manufacture of cloth was specially prohibited in the colonies. Flax seed, sheep, and tools for cloth manufacture when shipped into the colonies were labeled contraband. The shipper, carrier, and receiver could be prosecuted for smuggling, if caught. Wheelrights[1] and other artisans who made tools for the manufacture of cloth were excluded from all emigration lists. These men if caught trying to go to the colonies were given severe jail sentences. If caught a second time they were classed as criminals and faced with the possibility of losing a hand or their lives.

Cloth Manufacture in America

However, regulations and restrictions could not be executed effectively so far from England. Smugglers succeeded in satisfying the demand for flax seed and sheep. Tool makers were willing to take the risk of jail sentences when success meant they could secure the greater business profits offered by the colonists. A greater number of these men slipped through the patrols than were apprehended and punished. Because of this, the cloth industry in the northern colonies was so far advanced that by the year 1640 the court of Massachusetts passed two orders. The first gave a substantial bounty to the colonists most skillful at breaking,[2] spinning, and weaving flax. The second order created classes in the art of linen-making for young boys and girls. Connecticut, as well as New Hampshire, soon followed with similar laws.

A few sheep were brought to the colonies of Virginia and Massachusetts by the earliest settlers before England realized the threat to her own woolen industry. By careful guarding and

---

[1] The name originally signified men who made spinning wheels and wagon wheels.

[2] A term used to indicate one phase of linen manufacture.

nurturing of the original stock, plus interbreeding new stock smuggled into the colonies from time to time, the herds were soon prospering.

The colonies, almost from the beginning, passed many varied laws to encourage the cloth industry. Common grazing lands were set aside in most towns. In some New England villages, a town shepherd was hired with public monies to care for the villagers' flocks. The export of live sheep was forbidden, as was the slaughter for sale of any sheep under two years of age. Any dog that killed a sheep had to be hanged and his owner compelled to pay double indemnity to the sheep's owner. Each family was required to have one full-time spinner. All persons not otherwise employed (boys, girls and unmarried women) were required by law to do a certain amount of spinning each day. In Virginia, the Assembly was informed by certain authorities (probably the first investigation committee in America) that thirty people could be clothed from the combined efforts of five children and not over thirteen years of age. The Assembly later passed a resolution authorizing the county courthouses to pay six pounds of tobacco—tobacco was legal tender in most colonies—to any resident who brought in one yard of homespun, woolen cloth grown and woven by his own family. Since each family in the south had to import its own necessities from London, and since tobacco and a few other field crops were the only payment London merchants could accept, those who devoted their time to making things needed for colony consumption had to be paid from the public treasury.

In 1642 a book called *New England's First Fruits* was printed. It said in part:

> "With cotton woll[1] which we have at reasonable rates from the islands[2] and our linnen yarne, we can make dimities and fustians for our summer cloathing; and having a matter of 1,000 sheepe which prosper well, do begin withal, in a competent time we hope to have woolen cloath there made."

[1] Cotton.
[2] Bermuda and the West Indies.

The Fustian mentioned here was not the cloth presently known by that name, corduroy or velveteen, but a far coarser, rougher cloth with a flax or "tow"[1] warp and a shaggy, loosely-twisted cotton woof.[2] Dyed, usually blue, and pressed; it was worth one shilling a yard in 1640. This was one of the first types of cloth loomed in the New World because of its well-known wearing qualities. Throughout the Middle Ages it was worn by the peasants and working people in general, especially in the monasteries where it was used for so long a time that it acquired the name of monk's cloth.

One other half-linen cloth made widely during colonial times, and indeed used for work clothing until quite recent times, was a linen-warp, wool-woof cloth known as linsey-woolsey. It is best known because it was worn as a part or all of many of the volunteer uniforms during the Revolutionary War. Dyed a brown color with homemade butternut dye, it was made into shirts and sometimes even trousers for the farmer recruits. Its greatest advantage lay in the economic fact that both the linen and wool could be grown, spun, and loomed on the same farm. Cotton was largely imported from the Caribbean Islands and Egypt before Eli Whitney invented the cotton gin in 1793 when it became economically feasible to grow cotton as a field crop.

It would seem that all this industry would have produced more than enough cloth for the young colonies. The contrary was true, however. One full year was needed to grow a crop of flax and do the arduous tasks needed to prepare it for the spinning wheel. The spinning, winding the yarn into skeins, and bleaching took another full year. It then took months of patient weaving on the big looms before the flax could be called linen. From sixty to three hundred threads per square inch were required depending on the coarseness or fineness of the yarn. Then followed the drying and pressing before the cloth was suitable for use. A similar length of time was also

[1] Another name for flax.
[2] Warp threads run the length of the cloth. They were strung on the loom. Woof threads run the width of the cloth and were woven between the warp threads with a shuttle.

required for woolen cloth, woolen-linen, and linen-cotton mix-tures previously discussed. When the above facts are considered it may be readily understood why for over a hundred years from the first colonial settlement all or almost all the cloth manufactured or imported was needed for clothing. There was a very small quantity of cloth remaining that could be used to make the European type of quilt. The colonists' production of cloth together with all the cloth imported from England was not adequate to comfortably clothe the entire colonial popula-tion. England passed more and more laws in the endeavor to restrict the colonial cloth industry. It was not until the indus-trial revolution made cloth easier and faster to produce that this situation was alleviated.

The First Crazy Quilts

When the quilts and blankets which the colonists brought with them began to wear out, they must have been patched until the cloth would no longer hold thread. They were then probably replaced by quilts closely resembling our crazy-quilts —made from pieces of material of miscellaneous sizes, shapes and colors. Of course none of these quilts have survived the more than three centuries that have passed since they were made. Also, no one took the trouble to describe these early quilts in the journals, letters, and wills which mention them. It can only be surmised from what is known of the conditions existing at that time, how the quilts made by the earliest co-lonial women must have looked. These quilts could not have been very pretty because they were contrived from the strong pieces cut out of otherwise unusable clothing. Therefore, the quilts were more a result of accident than of design.

Tied Quilts

Some Pilgrim woman, name unknown, patched together the scraps left from the cutting table after her garments were cut

2. *The predominantly blue and brown prints used in this Melon Patch quilt show that it must have been made around 1850. (Woodrow Wilson Birthplace Foundation, Inc., Staunton, Virginia.)*

out. This was the origin of the American quilt. The quilt was filled with grasses or corn husks, and instead of beautiful quilting—the colonists had neither the time nor materials for this—string tied in knots at intervals held the top, bottom, and stuffing together. Short pieces of twine were put through the quilt with a needle, leaving both ends of the twine on the front of the quilt. These ends were then tied in a knot and the ends clipped off.

Early American Quilt Colors

To the Pilgrim women who were accustomed to woven blankets and finely-quilted coverlets, these quilts must have looked like sorry makeshifts. But the quilts were warm, and that was all that mattered at that time. However, they were not black, white and gray as some of the earlier historians would have us believe. They mistook the early English phrase "sad colors" to mean the colors worn at funerals. What the seventeenth century expression actually meant was dark colors. The Pilgrms wore the so-called sad colors of dark red, dark blue, dark green, dark brown, black and dark gray, both for work and for dress occasions. The other colonists or "worldly" people wore bright colors except when working, at which time the sad colors were worn. These people were too near to the Middle Ages, with their inherent love of bright colors, to be able to forego colors entirely.

Pieced Quilts

In the settled section, the necessity for pioneering plainness slowly gave way to a more leisurely comfortable way of life. At this time the housewives began to take more pride in the making of their scrap quilts. They took more care in blending the colors to make them more pleasing to the eye. Then followed the cutting of scraps into squares which wasted a little of the cloth, but gave a more orderly appearance to the quilt.

3. *Modern appliquéd quilt patterns like this one consist of sprays of flowers scattered regularly over the top with a wreath of flowers for a border. (From a quilt owned by Mrs. Sara Nolph.)*

Women began to take real pleasure in making this new kind of quilt. Each became a challenge to them as they tried newer and more intricate designs and pleasing color combinations.

The American patchwork quilt had been born and became a definite branch of quilt-making. It was one of the first new arts of the New World which contributed to the culture of the Old World. It is truly an American craft, deeply imbedded in American customs. In Colonial times quilt-making was so popular that it led to the making of the elaborate piece-work and appliqué quilts we admire in museums and historic restorations such as Mt. Vernon and Williamsburg.

Indeed, the interest in quilts and quilting shows no evidence of dying out.

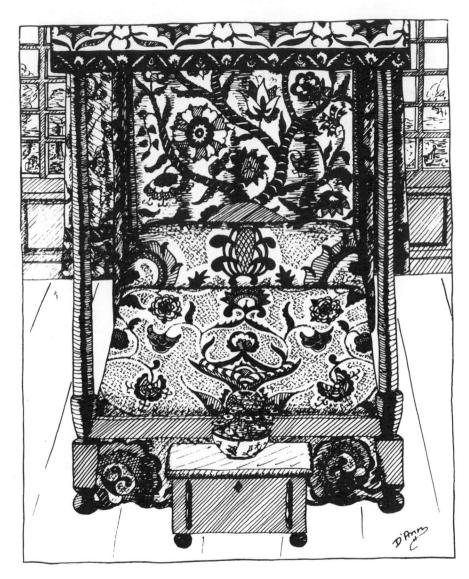

4. *A design of a seventeenth century crewel-work quilt and hanging. (Based on those at "Wakefield," George Washington's Birthplace National Monument, Washington's Birthplace, Virginia.)*

II

A DICTIONARY OF
QUILTING TERMS

ALL-QUILTED QUILT is made of two large pieces of fabric, either plain or printed, with filler between. If the cloth used was plain-colored or white, an elaborate design was drawn on the top and then quilted. When a printed fabric was used, the design printed on the cloth was quilted with the main elements stuffed and padded to stand out from the background.

ALL-WHITE QUILT is made from two sheets of white cloth with a filler between. It is elaborately quilted with white thread and requires considerable skill at hand sewing since there is no color, figure or pattern to distract the eye from the stitches themselves. With the advent of the sewing machine and the decline in hand sewing, the number of all-white quilts has diminished; the only examples of all-white quilts made in the last sixty years that I have been able to find are the small crib quilts made by fond grandmothers and a few talented mothers for the first baby. However, knowledgeable quilters have long considered it the most beautiful and elegant of all quilts.

APPLIQUE QUILT: Appliqué comes from the French word *appliquer* meaning *put on* or lay on as figures cut from one fabric and sewed to another larger piece of fabric.

BACKING (1) is the bottom layer of the quilt made of unbleached muslin or cotton sheeting which is white in most quilts although it may also be printed cotton fabric or a solid pastel shade.

BACKING (2) is also used to designate the square or block of cloth which backs a patch.

BINDING (noun): The material used to finish the edge around a quilt. It could be tape, or strips cut on the bias.

BINDING (verb): To cover the edges of the three layers and hold them together. It is the finishing of a quilt.

BLIND STITCH: See Hemming.

BLOCK is one complete pattern in fabric. It could be one cut piece of material one-half inch square in size to a piece of material large enough to cover a bed. It may be any number of pieces of fabric sewed together as long as it forms one complete pattern.

A COMFORTER: In the last forty years the name comforter has been given to a factory-made quilt of satin or nylon, over-stuffed by quilting standards. This kind of quilt is three to four inches thick in comparison to one-fourth inch thick for a normal quilt. It is loosely machine-stitched in large figures with wide spaces between them. Variant: means a tied quilt in the West.

CORNER BLOCK is used in a border to turn a corner.

COUNTERPANE: Rather an old-fashioned name for bedspread, often applied to a quilt or other covering used as a spread.

COVERLET: Used on bed primarily for warmth, is not large enough to cover the pillows. Until recently the most popular quilt size.

CRAZY QUILT: A top made of pieces of cloth in various sizes, shapes, colors and possibly materials sewn together like a jigsaw puzzle.

CREWEL-WORK: See entry following.

EMBROIDERED OF CREWEL-WORK QUILTS: In Europe, these were made on heavy linen with the same designs that were used in embroidered spreads, the only difference between them being the quilting. The quilt is started just like an elaborately quilted quilt but it has open spaces left in the quilting design which were filled in with crewel-work designs. Fig. 4 is an example of a seventeenth century embroidered quilt and its hangings. Since this quilt is one that takes expert quilting, an artistic eye, and a great deal of time and patience, the existing examples, no matter how recently made, are very valuable.

THE EUROPEAN QUILT OF EARLY DAYS: The beauty of this type of quilt was in the design. The top was a piece of patterned fabric, appliquéd in a continuous sheet or a plain-colored cloth. An elaborately printed chintz of either flowered or scenic design was chosen as the appliqué, while velvet or silk might be the background. The background of the chintz was cut away and only the designs themselves were appliquéd onto the background material. The quilting was still of first importance, bringing out the pattern of the chintz or making it recede into the background as the quilter wished.

American women began changing the appliquéd quilt almost as soon as it reached this country. First they cut out the designs from printed chintz into pieces of a more manageable size rather than use a full sheet. The next step was to cut individual printed elements from the chintz, as flowers, birds, or butterflies, and combine these elements into compositions of their own. At last they ignored the designs printed in the fabric and began to cut out their own design elements, making a leaf shape from green cloth, perhaps, a rose shape from pink fabric, etc. These design elements were then appliquéd on fabric squares.

FELL: Colloquial variant, see Hemming.

FILLER is the middle layer of a quilted quilt consisting of cotton, wool, or one of the new synthetic batts. In tied quilts the filler may be a woven blanket or length of flannel. Colloquial variant: wadding, stuffing.

HEMMING is to fold and sew down the edge of; making small slanting stitches from right to left catching only a thread or two under the material. Blind hemming (or stitching) is done like hemming but with larger stitches through the fold and only one thread on the right side.

HEXAGON QUILTS are pieced quilts, but there are things about them that are unique enough to place them in a category of their own. Strictly American—there is no record of them in Europe—they have been in existence for as long as records of quilts have been kept in the colonies and the United States but where they came from, or when, is a mystery. Hexagon quilts are beautiful, but very hard to make. A hexagon is made by cutting a right triangle from each corner of a square leaving a figure with six equal sides. There are several quilt patterns made from hexagons, the most common one being Grandmother's Flower Garden. Much care is needed in the sewing of a hexagon quilt to make each of the six corners a sharp point and each of the six sides a straight line on each piece. Because of their great beauty, in spite of the need for painstaking work, more hexagon quilts are being pieced today than any other single type of pieced quilt.

ITALIAN QUILTING: See Trapunto Quilting.

MARKING A QUILT: The act of drawing the quilting design onto either the top or the backing preparatory to quilting.

MASTERPIECE QUILTS: Prestige symbols are almost as old as mankind. Every generation has its own symbols that mean more than anything else in the world to it. For most of the history of the United States, a fine quilt, handmade by the owner, was the finest status symbol of all.

The Masterpiece Quilt most often seen is the Lone Star or Star of Bethlehem. This is a star of diamonds that covered the entire top of the quilt (Frontispiece). It was very difficult to piece. All of the points must be in perfect alignment and care must be taken to make the top lie perfectly flat. One diamond sewn a trifle off center could put a pucker in the top, thus spoiling the whole quilt. Nevertheless, a great many of these quilts have been made because of the prestige they give the owner.

In the Middle and Far West the appliquéd quilts were considered so difficult an accomplishment that they were made as masterpiece quilts—as evidence that a lady was an expert

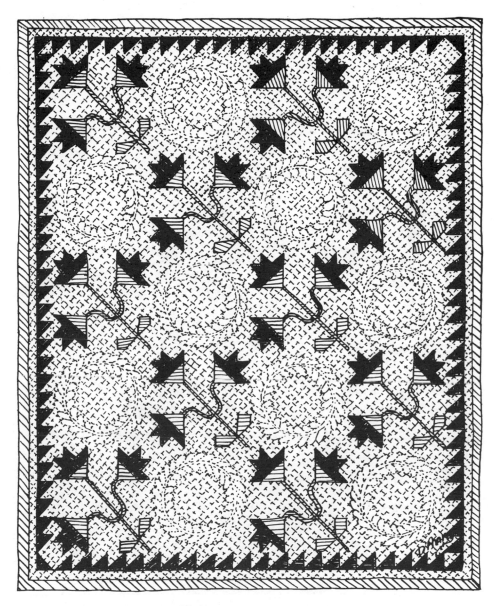

5. *A favorite of the nineteenth century was the red and green on white Double Tulip quilt. This was copied from a quilt at least 100 years old (owned by Mrs. Retha Gambaro).*

6. *Single Irish Chain in soft faded red and green on white. (From a quilt and stand with wash set at the Woodrow Wilson Birthplace Foundation, Inc., Staunton, Virginia.)*

needlewoman. A lady made piece-work quilts until she was sure of her craft. Then when she felt she had developed sufficient skill she began either a Horn of Plenty with fruit and flowers spilling out of the horn into clusters and sprays all over the quilt top, or perhaps a Garden Wreath that was an all-over spray of flowers. When these quilts were exhibited at the county fair everyone knew that the lady was a master needlewoman.

All of these masterpiece quilts could be worked on only when the quilter was rested and the light good. Before the electric light was invented, women used to start two quilts at the same time, one a masterpiece the other a utility quilt. The utility quilt could be a crazy quilt, or any other top that would use up the scraps left after cutting the pieces for the masterpiece quilt. Also the seamstress could work on this quilt when she was tired or the light too poor for her best efforts.

MEDALLION QUILTS: Such quilts may be either pieced or appliquéd. A medallion quilt is made by choosing a central motif that may be a piece of picture chintz, an appliqué or embroidered picture, or even something like a commemorative handkerchief. Anything made of cloth will serve as a central theme for a quilt, because this quilt should tell a story no matter how simple. When the central theme picture is ready, strips of pieced or appliquéd materials must be added to the central motif, one at a time, to form concentric rings. The strips may have corner blocks that help convey the story of the quilt. The strips usually vary in width, tending to get wider as they reach the outer circumference of the quilt. A medallion quilt calls for great taste and skill in balancing the colors included, the size of the central motif, and the size of the strips. But to an experienced needlewoman making this type of quilt could be a thrilling challenge resulting in a lovely work of art.

MITRE A CORNER: To turn a 90° corner with diagonal seam made from the inside corner to the outside corner of the strip.

PADDED WORK is to raise a portion of a quilting design by adding more cotton to the filler through the backing.

PATCH: As noun, used interchangeably with piece, or block. As verb, refers to the act of piecing a quilt, and also to appliqué. One of the most misused and misunderstood words in quilting.

PATCHWORK QUILTS: Same as appliquéd quilts; also used when referring to the entire subject of quilt-making.

PIECE: As noun, a small section of cloth that goes to make up a patch. As verb, to sew sections of cloth together into a patch.

PIECED AMERICAN QUILTS: The first development of American quilting from the crazy quilt was the pieced quilt, and at least seventy-five per cent of all quilts made by American women since have been pieced from material cut into geometric shapes. It seems likely that the housewife, after cloth became a little easier to obtain, would think of cutting the quilt pieces into squares. Squares are easier to sew together and make a neater quilt top. By mixing or matching colors, a variety of pleasing patterns can be made. Four-patches, nine-patches and also most of the other designs using squares were probably first made at this time. There are many variations that can be made by just using squares. Women tried most of them before discovering the almost limitless patterns that can be made by cutting the squares in halves or quarters and sewing them together in different forms. Squares, triangles, and diamond shapes (which are two triangles sewn together end to end) were combined. The ladies in the eighteenth century had almost as much variety in their quilt patterns as exists today. There remained only one more thing for the ladies to learn, how to piece a curve. It is not known who discovered that curves could be pieced in a manner which enabled them to lie flat enough for a quilt top, but it was some time after the middle of the eighteenth century.

The first patterns with curved pieces in them are dated just prior to or after the Revolutionary War. All of the pieced quilt patterns we use today are based on these three devices: squares, triangles, and curves. The ingenuity that created these patterns is not exhausted. There are still hundreds of ways to combine these three forms into quilt patterns that have never before been used.

A PUFF: See Comforter. Colloquial variant: a tied quilt in New England.

QUILT: (Noun) A quilt top, filling and backing, sewed together around the edges and over the whole body of the coverlet. (Verb) The act of stitching three layers of a quilt together in decorative designs.

QUILT TOP: The main sheet of material used in a quilt. It may be pieced, appliquéd, embroidered, or decorated in any manner, as long as it is used as the upper portion of a quilt.

REVERSE APPLIQUE is a type of appliquéing where the figure is cut from the background of the appliqué patch and a patch of contrasting color is applied to the back of the backing. The backing is turned and hemmed to the smaller patch.

A THROW is a coverlet just large enough to cover the top of a mattress. It is called a throw because it is thrown over a person who is napping. An afghan is the most common form of throw. However, the subject of this book is bedcovers which are quilted.

TIED QUILT: A quilt top and backing with a woven filler or without a filler. These are fastened together with yarn knots at intervals over the whole body of the coverlet.

TRAPUNTO QUILTING is a high-relief decorative design worked through two or more layers of material by outlining the design in running stitches and padding it from the underside. Orlon bulky yarn should be used as padding rather than wool for clothing and household articles that might be washed in hot water.

UTILITY QUILT: See Masterpiece Quilt.

VICTORIAN CRAZY QUILT: A quilt top made in the manner of an ordinary crazy quilt but of silk, satin, velvet, lace, and other exotic fabrics. Generally heavily embroidered with pictures and each piece outlined with embroidery stitches. Popular 1870-1900.

WHIP: See Hemming.

7. *Double Irish Chain in green and red on white with a Rambling Rose border. The quilt is named The Lancaster Rose because the cloth was brought from Lancaster, England, in 1800. (Star Spangled Banner House, Baltimore, Maryland.)*

III

QUILT NAMES

No record remains of the first quilt names, nor the patterns to which they were given, but naming quilts is a custom as old as quilt-making. Slang, popular sayings, and customs of the day, as well as the familiar everyday tools and objects around the house, were all reflected in the names given to quilts. These names give us an insight into the everyday life of another era that is difficult to find in any other way.

Quilts Named for Familiar Objects

Here is pictured the Sugar Loaf (Fig. 8) just as it used to come from the grocer's shelf before sugar was granulated. Its wrapper is blue because all sugar cones were wrapped in blue paper for shipment. This paper was saved very carefully because it was used in the dyepot, and gave cloth a very pretty blue color. The sugar loaf has been gone from the grocery shelf for the last seventy-five years. This pattern is at least that old and is perhaps much older.

The Oriole Window, that pinnacle of high style in the 1870s, was sewn into a quilt and shines as brightly today as the glass ones did in the last century (Fig. 9).

Milady's Fan (Fig. 10) flutters brightly in many different quilt patterns, and Tangled Garters peek brazenly forth from another (Fig. 11). Almost any object or expression suggested

37

8. *Sugar Loaf*   9. *Oriole Window*   10. *Milady's Fan*   11. *Tangled Garters*
12. *Blue Blazes,* also called *Honey Bee*   13. *Pure Symbol of Right Doctrine,*
also called *Mound Builders* and *Wind Power of the Osage*   14. *Eagle and Banner*
15. *Eagle and Flag*   16. *Eagle*   17. *George Washington and Colonial Soldier*
18. *Thirteen Stars*   19. *Laurel Wreath*

names. The ladies were not slow to use catchy slang phrases in their patterns. The expressions Blue Blazes (Fig. 12) and the Quaker phrase "The Pure Symbol of Right Doctrine" (Fig. 13) are significant examples. It is interesting to find a swastika in quilt designs because it is one of the oldest of good-luck symbols. This emblem has been found among every people as far back as the Stone Age. The Greeks had the swastika as well as the American Indians, to name two widely divergent peoples. So it is wrong to feel that the swastika represents Fascism; it has been warped into that evil only in the last fifty years.

Patriotic and Political Motifs

War or sudden political events brought on a rash of quilt patterns. These were usually old patterns renamed and were highly patriotic in theme. Eagles, stars, appliquéd soldiers, and many other patriotic motifs (Figs. 14-19) were introduced into the basic patterns to justify the new names of quilts. Enthusiastic quilters, always eager for new patterns, scanned dramatic incidents for fresh inspirations. They hurried to finish their quilts before the event or personage faded into history and some new bit of news became the talk of the sewing circle. Thus the ladies showed political bias on their beds long years before they received the voting franchise. It may be surmised that some otherwise meek woman kept silent to her staunch Whig husband that he was sleeping under a Democrat Rose (Fig. 20). In fact, during the Jackson-Adams Presidential Campaign in 1824, political opponents actually came to blows over whether a pattern similar to Fig. 21 was a Democrat Rose or a Whig Rose. It seems that these two patterns grew more and more alike, to the extent that when tempers grew uncertain over the candidates' affiliations, even the similarities of the quilt patterns were brought into the fight. It is interesting to note that it was men, not women, who fought over this quilt pattern.

Some famous patterns with political names are listed below.

20. *Democrat Rose* 21. *Democrat or Whig Rose* 22. *The Lobster* 23. *Burgoyne Surrounded* 24. *54-40 or Fight* 25. *Lincoln's Platform* 26. *The Little Giant* 27. *Washington's Quilt* 28. *Jackson's Star* 29. *Hawaiian Grape Vine* 30. *Philadelphia Pavements* 31. *Georgetown Circles*

The Lobster (Fig. 22) which was named for a fancied resemblance to that creature, was developed along the seacoast very early in the colonial period. It became generally popular in all fifteen states following the British attack on the Capitol at Washington, D.C. during the War of 1812. As Lobsterback was the popular derisive nickname for the red-coated British soldiers, it was considered a rebuff at England to use The Lobster with eagles, five-pointed stars, and other American symbols. "Burgoyne Surrounded" (Fig. 23) commemorates the Battle of Yorktown and the successful ending of the Revolutionary War. 54-40 or Fight (Fig. 24) was made popular by the quarrel with British Canada over the division of the Pacific Northwest in 1846. For some strange reason this pattern, unlike most other politically inspired ones has retained both its popularity and its name, unchanged after more than one hundred years.

The Lincoln-Douglas debates in 1854, caused the ladies to choose sides over the patterns Lincoln's Platform (Fig. 25) and The Little Giant (Fig. 26). The latter pattern is one of the few named for a losing presidential candidate that did not disappear following the election.

Presidential elections, of course, were the occasions for naming patterns for the candidates. There are many of such patterns ranging from Washington's Quilt (Fig. 27), Jackson's Star (Fig. 28), and Henry of the West (named for William Henry Harrison), Tippy Canoe and Tyler, Too (named for John Tyler), to the latest one, the Roosevelt Rose. The last-named pattern was made by a lady living in Washington, D.C. for Franklin D. Roosevelt.[1] She was chosen by the ladies' political club because of her fine needlework. Before Roosevelt's election it was the custom to present each president with a quilt shortly after his inauguration but this custom has completely died out and the Roosevelt Rose is the last presidential quilt made.

---

[1] This information was given to me by a very reliable source, but the Roosevelt Foundation can find no record of the quilt.

Inspiration from Places and Events

Each of the states has many quilt patterns named for it.
Hawaii, the last state to enter the Union, has at least one, The
Hawaiian Grape Vine (Fig. 29). Quilting was taken to Hawaii
by the early missionaries. It took deep root in the islands
along with the mother-hubbard dress which was introduced at
the same time.

Many cities are likewise honored by quilt names; Philadelphia Pavements (Fig. 30), Georgetown Circles (Fig. 31), Chicago Star (Fig. 32) are selected as representative.

Historical events are depicted in such titles as Charter Oak
(Fig. 34), Sherman's March, and Whig Defeat (Figs. 35, 36).

The westward expansion of our country was acknowledged
by such names as Road to Oklahoma (Fig. 37), Crossed Roads
to Texas (Fig. 38), and Rocky Road to Kansas (Fig. 39).

The hardships of the pioneer were commemorated in Trail
of the Covered Wagon (Fig. 40) and Kansas Dugout (Fig. 41).

The social life of the country was indicated by names as
varied as Temperance Tree (Fig. 42), Mrs. Morgan's Choice
(Fig. 43), and Four-H Club Patch (Fig. 44). The pattern
Drunkard's Path (Fig. 206) was offset by pattern W.C.T.U.
(Fig. 45).

Events that were not historic but captivated the people's
fancy were also exploited for quilt patterns. The Tail of Benjamin's Kite (Fig. 40) is an amusing one, while Steeple Chase
(Fig. 214) reminds one of an exciting time. The square dance
gave us names like Eight Hands Round and Swing in the Center (Figs. 79 and 80).

All fairs held quilt contests. However, the world's fairs have
the largest contests where high honors are bestowed upon the
winners. The author possesses two quilt patterns that won the
blue ribbons in past world fairs. The first is a pattern from a
quilt that won first prize at the World's Columbian Exposition,
at Chicago in 1893 (Fig. 46). The other is a winner of the
New York World's Fair in 1939. This quilt, made by a Washington, D.C. woman named Mrs. Jo-Ro-Betts, has been exhibited in more countries of the world than any other American
quilt.

32. *Chicago Star* 33. *California Plume* 34. *Charter Oak* 35. *Sherman's March*, also called *Hole in the Barn Door* 36. *Whig Defeat*, also called *Grandmother's Engagement Ring* 37. *Road to Oklahoma* 38. *Crossed Roads to Texas* 39. *Rocky Road to Kansas* 40. *Trail of the Covered Wagon*, also called *Tail of Benjamin's Kite* 41. *Kansas Dugout* 42. *Temperance Tree*, also called *Pine Tree* and *Tall Pine Tree* 43. *Mrs. Morgan's Choice*

44. *Four-H Club Patch*   45. *W.T.C. Union*   46. *World's Fair Quilt (1893)*
47. *Pullman Puzzle*   48. *Air Plane*   49. *Carpenter's Square*   50. *Cowboy's Star*   51. *Priscilla Alden*   52. *Barbara Frietchie Star*   53. *Dolly Madison Star* 54. *Martha Washington's Star*   55. *Mrs. Cleveland's Choice*

This country's past and present were indicated by Pullman Puzzle (Fig. 47), Air Plane (Fig. 48), Carpenter's Square (Fig. 49) and Cowboy's Star (Fig. 50).

Even the Indians were honored with patterns called Mound Builders (Fig. 13), Indian Hatchet (Fig. 96), which is a very old pattern, and Wind Power of the Osage (Fig. 13).

There were other ways a quilt might be named. The pattern itself might suggest the name like The Anvil or The Reel (Figs. 67, 68) which resemble those tools. And some names seem to be pure whimsy; for example, The Brown Goose (Fig. 71), Hairpin Catcher (Fig. 99) and Hole in the Barn Door (Fig. 35) which have no apparent connection with the patterns.

Romance was represented by such names as Cupid's Arrow-point (Fig. 72) and Bridal Stairway (Fig. 73); its complications gave us The Eternal Triangle (Fig. 74); its culmination gave us the Double Wedding Ring (Fig. 126).

Interest in foreign countries gave us names like Dutch Mill (Fig. 75), Arabian Star (Fig. 76) and Chinese Puzzle (Fig. 77). One pattern was named Around the World (Fig. 212) and another World's Without End (Fig. 78).

In fact, there was little or nothing that could not suggest a pattern or a pattern name. As suggested by one quilt pattern, there were "All Kinds" (Fig. 97).

Religious Names

The most prevalent names among quilts were either religious or floral. Among the favorite religious names were Jacob's Ladder (Fig. 58), Joseph's Coat (Fig. 59), Rose of Sharon (Fig. 60), Star of Bethlehem (Frontispiece) and Garden of Eden (Fig. 61). Jacob's Ladder is a traditional pattern and is very seldom altered, either in name, shape, color, or manner of setting the blocks together. Navy blue and white is the usual color but quilts made in lighter blues have been seen. There are several designs known as Joseph's Coat but they are all similarly intricate and colorful. The Rose of Sharon quilt patterns are legion. Almost every pattern that has any resemblance to a rose has at one time or another been called Rose of Sharon. This is also the case with star patterns and their fancied association with the name Star of Bethlehem.

Names for Flora and Fauna

Flowers were used in such profusion that there is scarcely one that does not have a quilt pattern named for it. Among the flower names will be found: Ragged Robin (Fig. 84), which is the Colonial name for Garden Pink, the more familiar names Tulip, American Beauty Rose, Primrose Path, Morning Glory (Figs. 85 through 88), and Baby Aster (Fig. 89), Zinnia Border, and Mountain Laurel (Fig. 90).

The vegetable garden was remembered with the patterns, Corn and Beans, Strawberry Quilt, Melon Patch, and the Tobacco Leaf (Figs 91-94). One of the more unusual ones is the Pine Burr (Fig. 95) which reminds one of how close the woods were.

Birds, animals, and insects were mentioned in many quilt names, such as: Honey Bee (Fig. 12), Flying Swallows (Fig. 81), Spider Web (Fig. 82), Wild Goose Chase (Fig. 112), and Bear Tracks (Fig. 83).

Names for Favorite Heroines and Books

The ladies' heroines were not forgotten. There were quilt patterns named Priscilla Alden (Fig. 51), Barbara Frietchie Star (Fig. 52), Dolly Madison Star (Fig. 53), Martha Washington's Star (Fig. 54) and Mrs. Cleveland's Choice (Fig. 55).

One lady named a pattern for her mother. It has the unique name of Mary Tenny Grey Travel Club Patch (Fig. 56). There is even a patch named for that glamorous spy Madam X (Fig. 57).

Several patterns were named for popular fiction of their day. Scott's *Lady of the Lake* (Fig. 69) and Wallace's *Ben Hur* (Ben Hur's Chariot Wheel, Fig. 70), were honored in this way.

56. *Mary Tenny Grey Travel Club Patch*   57. *Madam X*   58. *Jacob's Ladder*
59. *Joseph's Coat*   60. *Rose of Sharon*   61. *Garden of Eden*   62. *Bailey's Nine-Patch*   63. *Olive's Yellow Tulip*   64. *Shoo-fly*   65. *Star Spangled Banner*
66. *Star of LeMoine*   67. *The Anvil*

68. *The Reel*   69. *Lady of the Lake*   70. *Ben Hur's Chariot Wheel*   71. *The Brown Goose*   72. *Cupid's Arrowpoint*   73. *Bridal Stairway*   74. *Eternal Triangle* 75. *Dutch Mill*   76. *Arabian Star*   77. *Chinese Puzzle*   78. *World's Without End* 79. *Eight Hands Round*

80. *Swing in the Center*   81. *Flying Swallows*   82. *Spider Web*   83. *Bear Track*
84. *Ragged Robin*   85. *Tulip*   86. *American Beauty Rose*   87. *Primrose Path*
88. *Morning Glory*   89. *Baby Aster*   90. *Mountain Laurel*   91. *Corn and Beans*

Misnomers and Regional Variations

A popular name was often applied to many patterns. Likewise a popular quilt pattern might have many names, each one correct for the particular time and locality. This practice of using a diversity of names for one quilt pattern could happen in a number of ways. Lavina might visit her Aunt Emma and be shown a quilt pattern that she wished to copy. At home perhaps she found that the name was already in use in her town. In this event she would deliberately change the pattern's name to avoid confusion. Or she may have forgotten the name and renamed it something like Aunt Emma's Choice. Bailey's Nine-Patch (Fig. 62) and Olive's Yellow Tulip (Fig. 63) are two examples of patterns renamed for quilters. Or maybe Lavina changed the colors of the original and decided to give hers a new name. This is the case of two patterns, the Shoo-fly (Fig. 64), and Star Spangled Banner (Fig. 65). The Shoo-fly is called by its regular name when done in any color combination except green and yellow on white; when pieced in these colors it is renamed Chinese Coin. The Star pattern done in red, white, and blue is Star Spangled Banner. When the pattern is copied in three shades of yellow it is Golden Splendor.

A perfect example of a pattern renamed many times but remaining basically unchanged is Fig. 5. The pattern started in New England as the Wood's Lily. It appeared next in Pennsylvania as the Pennsylvania Tulip; in the South as Mountain Lily and North Carolina Lily; in Ohio as the Tiger Lily; in Illinois as the Meadow Lily. Elsewhere in the Middle West it was known as the Double Tulip. The pattern crossed the Mississippi to become the Prairie Lily and ended its westward journey in California as the Mariposa Lily. It accomplished its long journey, which must have taken it a century or more, without changing its basic form.

An unusual way for a quilt to get its most common name is by a corruption of its original name. The basic diamond pattern for stars originated along the Mississippi River. It was named for The LeMoine brothers who explored the river for settlement and founded the city of New Orleans. It was called

92. *Strawberry Quilt*   93. *Melon Patch*   94. *Tobacco Leaf*   95. *Pine Burr*
96. *Indian Hatchet*   97. *All Kinds*

the Star of LeMoine (Figure 66). The pattern was very popular with the Americans who settled in the Mississippi Valley, and its name was gradually softened and shortened in the American language to Lemon Star. The pattern is known by both names today.

Some patterns have been lost and all that remains are their names. Two of these patterns, Candlelight and Lawyer's Puzzle were so popular that they were standards for quilters for over 100 years. Now after years of disuse not even a description remains. Perhaps the patterns are still in use, but they can no longer be identified by their original names.

98. *The blocks for this child's embroidered quilt were made during a 12-year-old boy's prolonged illness in the 1920s. His sister saved the blocks and made them into a quilt with red lattice strips. (Owned by Mrs. Permilla Codling.)*

IV

CLASSIFYING
PIECED QUILTS

When an art or craft exists for a long time, rules and conventions grow up around it. When the art or craft is in the category called folk art these rules are often uncertain or contradictory. The rules in the following chapter are those followed by generations of quilters trying to give order to their abstract and geometric designs. Where the rules were contradictory I have tried to straighten out the difficulties without violating tradition. There are four classes of pieced quilt patterns that have retained their popularity and three more that have become almost unused among quilters. There may have been more at one time but these less popular categories have disappeared along with the quilts made from them. Appliqué quilts cannot be classified except by subject, and since there are almost as many subjects as there are quilts it would be useless to attempt classification.

One-Patch Quilts

In this classification are all crazy quilts; medallion quilts; hexagon quilts; simple block designs, where no effort is made to separate the fabric by color or into smaller units; quilts made of pieces cut in a single size and shape; and any quilt that is pieced by starting in one corner and adding single pieces until the quilt is the correct size and shape.

99. *Hit or Miss,* also called *Hairpin Catcher* 100. *Brick Wall* 101. *Coarse Woven Patch* 102. *Fine Woven Patch* 103. *Hexagon Patch* 104. *Star Hexagon* 105. *Streak of Lightning* 106. *Brick Pile* 107. *Clamshell* 108. *Friendship Quilt* 109. *Cross Patch* 110. *Arabic Lattice*

By the time a one-patch quilt is half finished it is so cumbersome and heavy that it has earned the reputation of being a lapful. The small low-seated, high-backed, armless rocking chair, known as a sewing rocker, was designed so that a woman making a one-patch quilt could spread part of the quilt on the floor to be relieved of most of its weight.

CRAZY QUILTS enjoyed a comeback in the years from 1880 through 1910. However, from lumpy utilitarian objects, they were transformed into the pride of the needlewoman, being made of silks, satins, and velvets. Each piece was not only feather-stitched around its outline, but often was embroidered with a bird, animal, butterfly, flower, or other fancy. The whole quilt was a masterpiece of skill, labor, and delicate stitches.

MEDALLION QUILTS (Fig. 381) seem to have been popular from around 1700 until 1830; a few have been made in recent years for exhibition at fairs. Old ones are very rare; most of those that have been preserved are now in museums.

HEXAGON QUILTS (Figs. 103, 104) are personal favorites. They are technically one-patch quilts, because each design in the quilt must be built up in separate blocks which are then fastened together. These blocks cannot be divided into any of the other categories. They must be treated as if they are not sewn together, but are one piece of cloth, making a hexagon a one-patch quilt.

Embroidery was used in conjunction with appliqué or piecework in many American quilts but few embroidered quilts, as such, were made until the Victorian Crazy Quilt became popular.

From about 1910 until 1950, the only embroidered quilts were made from stamped cotton squares that could be found in most store art departments. These squares came in many sets with flowers, birds and other popular motifs. Many had juvenile designs and these were used to teach embroidery to both boys and girls, especially during the long northern winters (Diagram 1). These quilts were often embroidered in dye-fast turkey-red thread bought in spools. A case is known where a baby quilt was made from squares made by the father and mother when they were children. The same red color was used by both children even though they were in different towns (Fig. 98). In the last thirty years the most popular motif for these stamped squares have been Birds of the States and Flowers of the States (Diagram 2).

In the national magazines there is a new movement to teach women different embroidery stitches and how to use these stitches in making up their own designs. Crewel-work is one of the embroidery techniques being retaught to American women (Diagram 3). Originally the traditional crewel-work patterns were taken from the patterns on Chinese dishes that were an innovation to Europeans in the sixteenth and seventeenth centuries. These patterns were copied on furniture, on wallpaper, in painted and printed fabrics, in fact anywhere that they could be fitted onto a surface. The earliest settlers used crewel-work embroidery almost exclusively because the wool, two-strand crewel yarn was easier to obtain than linen thread. As in everything else, regional differences, slight at first, became new arts in themselves. In Deerfield, Connecticut, a new embroidery evolved from the old crewel-work, using the same

Diag. 1   *Diag. 2*

Diag. 3

Diag. 4

patterns but taking inspiration from Dutch blue-white onion-ware, that in turn had taken its original inspiration from the original Chinese dishes. The ladies of Deerfield did their embroidery in shades of blue with accents of cinnamon (See Diagram 4).

Two-Patch Quilts

Two-patch quilts are of two types: quilts pieced in lengthwise strips; or patches that are cut in half, one half pieced in a pattern and the other half either plain or appliquéd.

The Wild Goose Chase (Fig. 112) is a good example of the first type of two-patch. There are many examples of the second type; in the case of the Pine Tree (Fig. 42) the trunk of the tree is appliquéd as are the flowers of the Basket patch (Fig. 113). The two-patch patterns seem to be a kind of catch-all category. Any pieced work designs that do not fall easily into one of the other categories are classified as a two-patch quilt pattern. There is a great variety of two-patch patterns.

111. *Birds in the Air*   112. *Wild Goose Chase*   113. *The Basket*   114. *Fannie's Fan*   115. *Tall Pine Tree*   116. *Forbidden Fruit*   117. *Moon Over the Mountain* 118. *The Farmer's Wife*   119. *Queen Charlotte's Crown*   120. *Single Irish Chain* 121. *Double Irish Chain*   122. *Triple Irish Chain*

Three-, Five-, and Seven-Patch Quilts

The three-, five-, and seven-patch quilt patterns are very rare except for one five-patch pattern called Irish Chain (Figs. 120-122), which was pieced in single, double, and triple. Otherwise none of the other three-, five-, and seven-patch was ever very popular. In fact, many are completely lost except for tantalizingly vague hints in letters, journals, and elderly ladies' memories. All that can be determined are a few names and slight descriptions that do not give a clear picture of the quilt's appearance. However, the patterns I have so named are properly identified.

There are very few three-patch quilt patterns. They are distinguished by having only three pieces of cloth in each patch. Fig. 117 is a classic example of three-patch.

Five-patch patterns are divided into twenty-five squares, five across the top and five deep.

Seven-patch patterns are similar to five-patch patterns except that they have seven squares across, and seven deep.

Four-Patch Quilts

The four-patch is one of the most common bases for quilt patterns. It is not difficult to recognize a four-patch by simply measuring it. If a ruler shows that a pattern can be cut through the middle horizontally and vertically, leaving four identical patterns (two reversed), then the pattern is a four-patch. Diagram 5 shows the basic division that can be found in all four-patch patterns (Fig. 218-229). These basic shapes may be successively divided and redivided as long as they repeat the divisions exactly from the corners to the center. There are other four-patch patterns illustrated in some of the other drawings. It would be good practice to pick them out.

Some quilt patterns, Lone Star (Frontispiece) and Mariner's Compass (Fig. 228) to name two, may be enlarged so that one of the patches covers the entire quilt top, but these quilts still fit the definition.

Nine-Patch Quilts

Next to the four-patch, the nine-patch quilt patterns are the most popular and numerous. In these patterns the basic blocks may be divided in one of three ways: into nine equal squares (Diagram 6), into nine unequal blocks (Diagram 7), into the double nine-patch, where the middle and four corner squares are divided into nine equal squares or nine blocks (Diagram 8).

As has been indicated with the other types of quilts, these basic nine patches may be cut into more intricate shapes.

Where pieced blocks are set together with plain blocks, or lattice strips, the individual quilt patches are quite easy to pick out for identification. But where blocks are set together, it may take a little study to determine where one block ends and another begins. When confronted with this problem remember to include all parts of a design up to a repeat.

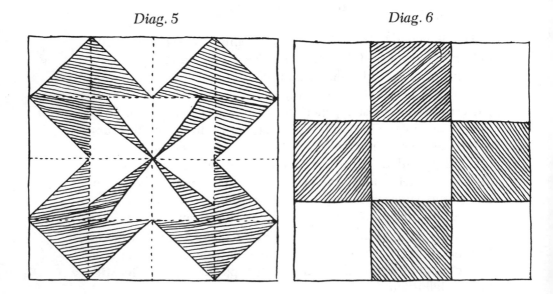

Diag. 5   *Diag. 6*

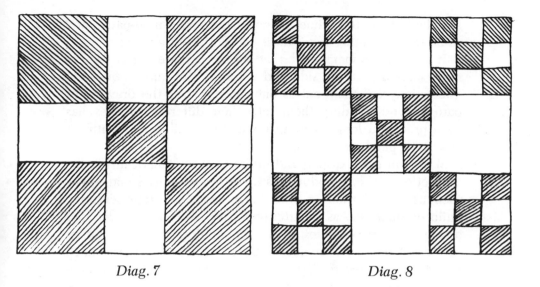

Diag. 7   Diag. 8

Patterns Half Piece and Half Appliqué

A quilt pattern that is half pieced, half appliquéd is grouped under the heading of the pieced half of the patch. Thus a Basket quilt (Fig. 113) is a two-patch quilt whether it has flowers on it or not. Diagrams 15 and 16 on page 87 show how one of these half-and-half quilt patterns is divided when the work is being done. The pattern called Double-Tulip has four Star of LeMoine minus one diamond each in the inside corners. This makes them Tulips instead of Stars to the quiltmaker. Since these Tulips are four-patches they make the whole quilt patch a four-patch in spite of the stems, leaves, and the rose appliquéd in the center of the patch.

Determining the Types

If after careful study the quilt classification cannot be determined, make sketches of a block on a piece of paper until one is the same size and shape as the quilt block. Draw lines of a four-patch pattern (the most common type) over the sketched block. If the lines do not match, try a nine-patch, and so on with the other types until you find the right one.

It must be remembered that where a pattern has two or more sections side by side and made of the same fabric, the quilter may cut them out as one piece. When the drawing of patterns and dividing them into their different patches has been practiced long enough, it will be possibly to identify a new quilt patch at a glance.

Many museums display old quilts in their American historical sections. The reproductions of historical houses and towns such as Mt. Vernon and Williamsburg have representative quilts on their beds as a matter of course. Much may be learned of the comparative dates of different quilt patterns by noting the age of the reconstructed bedroom and the quilt used in it. It is not surprising to find mistakes, however. Unless the decorator knows quilts or compares the age of the cloth used in the quilt with cloth he knows was used in that period he may believe that any pretty quilt will suffice. Quilt pattern styles change as popular taste changes but are revived at intervals in modified forms.

County fairs are, of course, traditional places to see fine exhibition quilts made by skilled needlewomen competing for prizes. At almost any county fair in the United States a few quilts may be seen, but if a person wishes to see large numbers of quilts, the fairs in the South and Middle West still have large numbers entered in their competitions each year.

Collecting Patterns

Our grandmothers used to make collections of quilt patterns. They would make up one block of each new quilt pattern that interested them. In this way they could make sure of not forgetting a pattern before they had time to piece it. They also had a nice selection to choose from when they wished to start a new quilt. A lady with a particularly choice collection would mention it in her will, giving it to a favorite daughter or niece. Collections of patterns were also made up as wedding presents.

A collection of quilt patterns, each measuring ten or twelve inches square, was certainly easier to store than a collection of whole quilts would have been. These single block collections were often saved from one generation to the next. If one were fortunate enough to live in an old house with an attic full of old trunks and chests of drawers, one might find such a collection tucked away in one of them. One lady I know found such a chest. It also contained quilt patterns cut from old newspapers. This was a double treasure, for the backs of those clippings were as fascinating as the front.

This old way of collecting quilt patterns is still practicable for one can increase one's knowledge of quilting without the bother and expense of making a whole quilt. Once a block of a new pattern is cut out and sewn, one can never be in doubt as to whether it is a four-patch or a nine-patch quilt.

123. *Handy Andy*   124. *Prickly Pear*   125. *Greek Cross*

126. *The Double Wedding Ring is not an old pattern; the earliest ones were made in the 1870s or 1880s.*

V

PIECING A QUILT TOP

The most difficult part of piecing a quilt is choosing a pattern. You may choose a traditional pattern or you might even design a new one. The color scheme has to be worked out, measurements taken of the bed (see chart for sizes, page 67). Then the fun of piecing a quilt begins.

Type of Materials

Always use new material. This cannot be overstressed. Quilts take time and work. They will last through many washings and years of service provided firmly woven, new materials of good quality are used. These materials may be the larger remnants left from dressmaking or new material bought expressly for the purpose.

Unbleached muslin, percale, or linen may be used for quilt backings as well as for background material for appliqué. If the length of material is not as wide as is needed, you may sew two pieces together lengthwise.

FOR APPLIQUE PATCHES AND PIECED SQUARES Use firmly woven cloth that will not fray. Drapery or upholstery materials called barkcloth and others of the same loosely woven type will pull loose from the thread used to sew the patches together, and will have to be replaced after the first washing. Frail, transparent, or semi-transparent materials are too fragile for quilts. Also, avoid denim, sailcloth, and other stiff, heavy cloths. Their coarse tex-

65

ture is unpleasant and they cannot be quilted as nicely as the softer fabrics. Fabrics that must be dry cleaned should not be used with washable cloth.

TEST ALL FABRICS by washing and ironing a small piece before the quilt pieces are cut out. Recent advances in cloth manufacture have almost eliminated the problems of shrinkage and non-fast colors, but if the small sample fades or shrinks, it is better to preshrink all the material than have the finished quilt pucker and break after the first washing. Running dye will ruin a quilt and make it unsightly. Red is a special offender which will turn a crisp red and white quilt to a drab rose and pink, it will turn blues to purple, or green to brown.

TO SET DYE IN CLOTH that shows a tendency to run add vinegar to boiling water and soak the cloth in this mixture for a few minutes before washing it. Use materials of the same weight and strength. Do not team heavy linen with fragile silk, nor heavy wool and cotton in the same quilt. The lighter fabrics will wear out first and leave holes in the quilt rendering it unusable, while the heavier materials will have many years of wear remaining.

A wool quilt may be backed with flannel. Always use new thread as thread on a spool may dry-rot as it ages.

Estimating Quantity of Material

MEASURE BED, DIAGRAM 9: Measure the bed to determine how much fabric will be needed. Beds come in standard sizes but there are many of these sizes and they can vary, especially if the bed is rather old.

Measure length of mattress from head to foot, width of mattress from side to side, depth of bed from the top of the mattress to the floor or dust ruffle.

The following chart gives standard bed and quilt sizes in inches. Adjust item if your bed is not a standard size. Twenty-two inches has been used as the average height of a bed and seventeen inches has been added to the length of the spreads to cover the pillows.

BED	MATTRESS MEASURES	BEDSPREAD		COVERLET	
		22" skirt	18" x skirt	22" skirt	18" skirt
TWIN	39" x 75"	83" x 114"	75" x 114"	83" x 97"	75" x 97"
DOUBLE	54" x 75"	98" x 114"	90" x 114"	98" x 97"	90" x 97"
KING	72" x 84"	116" x 123"	108" x 123"	116" x 106"	108" x 106"
COT	30" x 75"	74" x 114"	66" x 114"	74" x 97"	66" x 97"

*THROW SIZE IS 48" x 72"

QUEEN 60 x 80

96 x 116

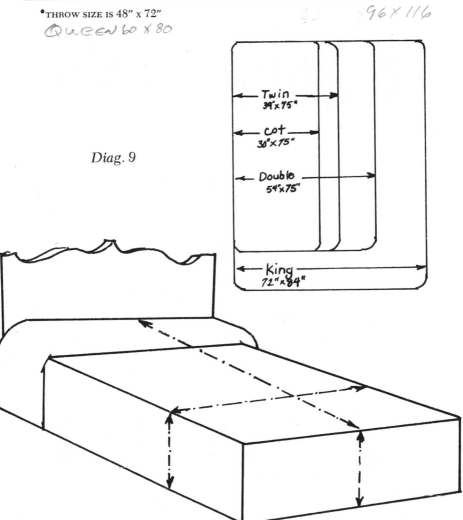

Diag. 9

Twin
39"x75"

cot
30"x75"

Double
54"x75"

King
72"x84"

Pick Quilt Type

BEDSPREADS: If the quilt is to be used primarily as a daytime cover, use the sizes indicated for a bedspread.

COVERLET: For a quilt to be used primarily for warmth at night. It does not cover the pillow since the excess 17 inches of quilt used in a spread are bulky and uncomfortable to a sleeper, also the added weight may cause the quilt to slide off the bed during the night. Be generous in your measurements, especially if the quilt is to be used by a large or heavy person.

THROW: A throw is usually four by six feet. This covers the form of a sleeping person without excess, and may be folded neatly at the foot of the bed when not in use.

Overall Dimensions

The size you will make the quilt will depend on whether you would like it to hang to the floor, to just below the top of a dust ruffle or petticoat, or whether it will be used on a free-standing bed with both sides of equal length, or a studio bed which has the back and side against a wall. If you have trouble deciding on the size you want, fold or pin a bed sheet until you like the result.

Again if the person who uses the quilt is larger or heavier than normal, be more generous in your measurements.

Estimating Yardage

FOR BACKING: To determine the amount of material needed, find the exact area in inches of your quilt. As an example the area of the double-bed bedspread with 18-inch skirt is 90 x 114 inches or 10,260 square inches. Translated into yards of 36-inch wide material this quilt would need six and two-thirds yards of muslin for backing. Not all of the muslin would be used; the length of the quilt requires three yards one foot of the muslin, the width requires a second piece the same length but 18 inches narrower than the first piece. The excess may be used in piecing the top.

FOR PIECED TOP: The amount of material needed for the top will depend on the pattern. The quilt will take the area of the backing in feet plus one-fourth inch per side of each piece in the pattern. Thus a pattern eight inches square will require a piece of material 9½ inches square if cut once diagonally. If cut in four equal blocks, it will require a 10-inch square of material, etc. Multiply the amount of material needed for a square by the number of blocks needed and you arrive at the amount of material needed for the quilt top. Divide this amount between the colors used for the pattern; if approximately half of the pattern is red, ¼ green and ¼ white, buy the material in those amounts. Remember there are 9 square feet in each square yard; thus if your pattern needs 8½ square feet of red cloth buy 1 square yard.

APPLIQUED TOP: To use the method detailed above for appliqué patterns measure each shape as if it were a square. A rose, with a one-inch diameter center, a two-inch inner circle of petals and a three-inch outer circle of petals would need a piece of cloth 3½ inches wide by 7½ inches long if all three pieces were to be cut from one color of material.

Choosing a Pattern

The choice of a pattern for a quilt is, of course, a matter of personal taste as are the colors used in the pattern. However, for a first or even a second quilt one of the simpler patterns like the four-patch or nine-patch would be easier. Then as you gain in skill and confidence a more complicated pattern could be attempted. Sometimes these simple patterns are more effective and pleasing than the more elaborate patterns. Also simple patterns in bright colors will go as well with the straight lines and limited ornamentation of modern designs as they do with Early American furniture.

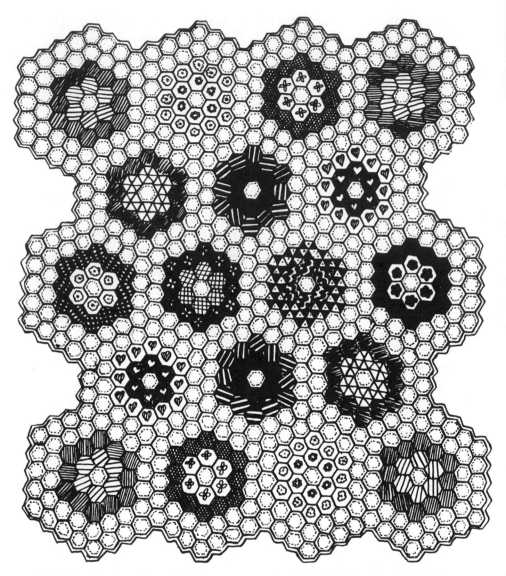

127. *The most popular of the hexagon patterns is called Grandmother's Flower Garden. All of the pieces have six equal sides and must be sewn with straight sides and sharp points. Even a slight mistake can throw the entire quilt out of alignment.*

What Size Patches?

You must now decide on the size to make the individual squares or patches. This is up to you, but 8-inch to 18-inch squares are generally favored. (Patches smaller than 8 inches add to the work of sewing; larger than 18 inches they become unwieldy.) An intricate pattern requires larger squares than a simple uncluttered pattern.

Suppose you have decided to make a full-length spread for a double bed. According to the chart above, you will need a quilt 90 x 114 inches. Ten-inch squares can be used—7 for the width and 9 for the length. This will allow ¼ inch for seaming the patches (as described on page 76). A difference of an inch

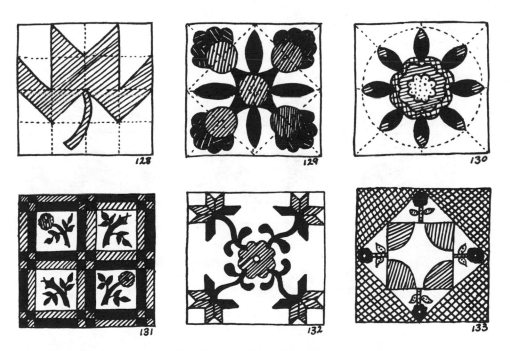

128. *Tulip Tree Leaves* 129. *Mexican Rose* 130. *Whig Rose* 131. *Framed Roses* 132. *Double Tulip* 133. *Spice Pinks*

134. *Conventional Swag Border*   135. *Swag and Tassel Border*   136. *Twisted Rope Border*   137. *Conventional Vine Border*   138. *Leaf and Grape Border* 139. *Tulip Border*   140. *Tulip Vine Border*

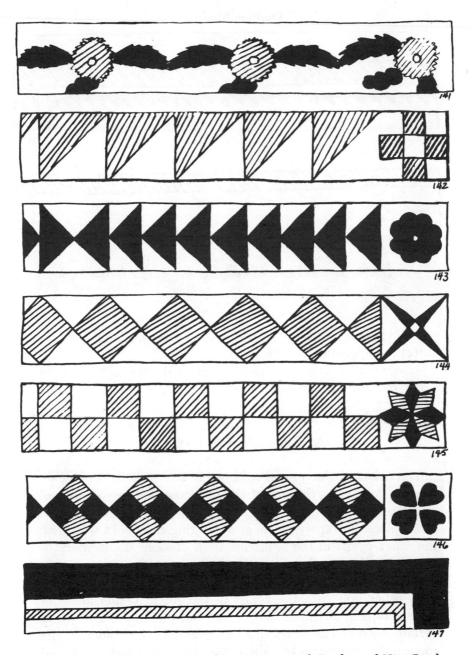

141. *Feather Spray with Leaf Border*   142. *Sawtooth Border and Nine-Patch Corner*   143. *Wild Goose Chase Border and Flower Corner*   144. *Chained Square Border and Star Corner*   145. *Checker-Board Border and Star Corner* 146. *Chained Four-Patch Border and Heart Corner*   147. *Triple Band Border*

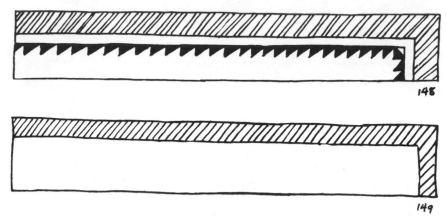

148. *Double Band and Sawtooth Border*　149. *Simple Bound Border*

or so whether in length or width is immaterial, and does not affect the appearance of the quilt.

If you decide to have a border, deduct the size of the border from the overall dimensions before figuring the patch sizes.

The Colors to Use

The colors in the quilt should be chosen with the same care used in decorating the rest of the bedroom. When you are uncertain, a simple device used by decorators may help you. Select a piece of drapery fabric or a painting that looks well with the other colors in the bedroom, then pick up the drapery or painting colors in the quilt. In this way you can be sure in advance that the quilt colors selected will harmonize with each other and with the colors in the room. Quilts made of dress scraps in all colors, both print and plain, also go well in certain rooms. The tones that complement the colors in the room will stand out while the other colors will fade back and be unnoticed. Patterns like the Double Wedding Ring (Fig. 126) or the Crazy Quilt, Grandmother's Flower Garden (Fig. 127) are good for such scrap quilts.

Equipment

When the overall pattern dimensions, sizes, border, and colors for the quilt have been decided upon, it is time to begin work on the quilt. You will need a large table, pencil, paper, cardboard, ruler, and of course, an eraser. For some patterns a compass for drawing circles will be required. Also the cloth, a book of small straight needles, several spools of number 50 or 40 thread, and a sharp pair of scissors.

Making a Crazy Quilt

You can get some idea of color possibilities by coloring a patch or two of the cardboard patterns with felt-tip markers or crayons. Or, even better, test a sample patch or two using the actual fabric.

The Crazy Quilt is the easiest of all quilts to piece. Scraps of cloth of all colors, shapes, and sizes are needed. These scraps are fitted together like a picture puzzle, with as little trimming as possible. If there are sewing scraps available, use them. If not, they may be obtained from anyone who sews and is willing to save the scraps. Most seamstresses are quite happy to find someone who will take their sewing scraps, because, like Christmas cards, it seems a shame to throw them away. Other likely places to obtain scraps are from the factory outlet of cotton mills. Also the yard goods departments of some department stores carry bundles of scraps for quilts or doll clothing that they obtain from dress manufacturers.

A crazy quilt can be made by either of two methods; both methods use unbleached muslin as a base for the scraps. By sewing these scraps to the muslin base there is no danger that the quilt will lose its shape or pucker when it is finished.

1. Obtain a piece of muslin the size of the desired quilt. If the muslin is not wide enough, sew two pieces to the proper width.

2. Select a patch having a right angle and place it in the upper left corner of the muslin.

3. Baste the patch to the muslin using long stitches along the side and top.

4. Leave the bottom and remaining side free.

5. Select a second patch having a straight edge, for the quilt's upper border, and a side which approximately fits into the outline of the free side of the first patch.

6. Place this patch face down, putting the two raw edges together.

7. Using ¼-inch seams, sew through the two patches and the muslin.

8. Turn the patch face out and baste the straight edge to the upper edge of the muslin.

9. Continue assembling patches on the muslin backing, sewing them to the patches previously placed as outlined in the steps above until the backing is completely covered.

Patches need not be unform—odd sizes and shapes make attractive patterns as long as each piece fits well along the edge of a previous patch and all raw edges are covered.

Leave at least ¼-inch seam on the patches as they are sewn. Utmost care must be taken as each patch is folded over to be tacked to prevent it or the muslin backing from stretching or puckering. Each piece must be laid back smoothly in order to ensure that the finished quilt will be the correct size and shape.

Alternate Method for Making a Crazy Quilt

This method is very similar to the first. Use muslin backing as before but cut it into 12 to 18-inch blocks. This eliminates the unwieldiness of the muslin cut from the first method. Sew the patches of material to the backing in the same way as in the first method. When all of the squares are finished, sew them together into a quilt top. This second method was very popular in Victorian times. The straight lines cutting through the irregular pattern gives the quilt a very different but not unpleasant appearance.

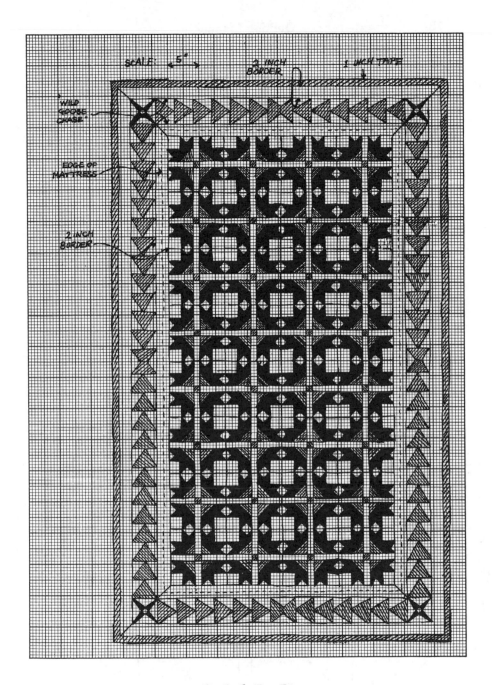

150. *Quilt Top Diagram*

Using Paper Backing

A very old way to make a crazy quilt and a method which recurs whenever there is a depression, as for example in the 1930's, was to use newspapers or other available paper instead of muslin to back the quilt patches.

Making a Pieced Top

Here are step-by-step details for making a quilt using Duck Paddle pattern with a Wild Goose Chase border (Fig. 150). The measurements are for a double bedspread with an 18″ overhang. The blocks are to be nine-inch squares; the colors red, white and green.

Diagram 10A. Draw a nine-inch square on cardboard. The cardboard put in men's laundered shirts is excellent. Always make your pattern in the exact size you will use in the quilt.

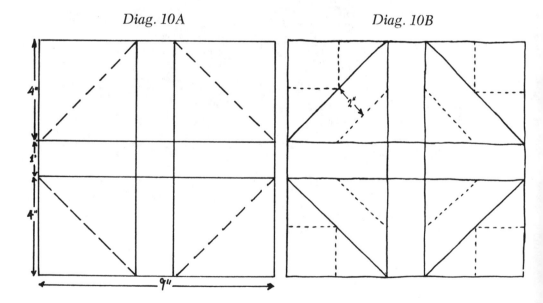

Diag. 10A   *Diag. 10B*

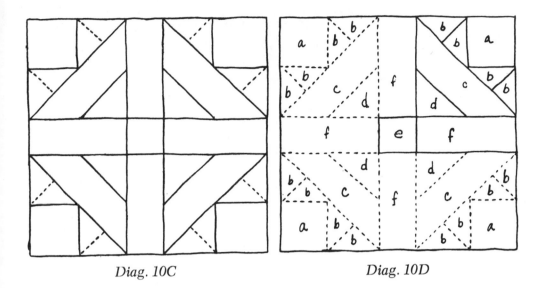

Diag. 10C   Diag. 10D

Draw two parallel lines one-inch apart, four inches from each corner. This makes a cross in the center. Draw diagonals across each of the four corners.

Diagram 10B. Draw another diagonal line two inches inside the first diagonal. Make a two-inch square in each corner.

Diagram 10C. Draw the lines as shown by dots.

Diagram 10D. You should now have four 2-inch squares (a); sixteen small triangles (b); four trapezoids (c); four large triangles (d); a 1-inch center square (e); and four rectangles (f).

Cut out and mark two or more cardboard models of each shape. When the first model loses its crisp edges and the points become round, change to a new model. A cardboard model if used too long will produce curved instead of straight lines, and round instead of pointed angles. (Women used to have their tinsmiths cut tin models for their quilts; then there was no danger of the patterns wearing out before the cutting of the pieces was finished. The pattern could also be given to others for the making of other quilts.)

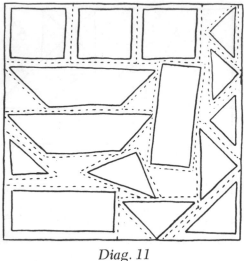

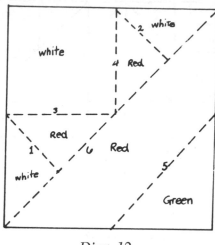

Diag. 11   *Diag. 12*

MARKING AND CUTTING,· DIAGRAM 11: The cloth should be ironed. Spread the cloth face down on a smooth table top or other cutting surface. Place the first pattern on one corner of the cloth, and trace around with a sharp pencil or white chalk, depending on whether the fabric is light or dark. Trace the second pattern ½-inch from the first one. This ½-inch margin, cut in half, will give you a ¼-inch hem or seam allowance for each piece. Retrace the pattern until you have all required pieces.

Cut out the pieces; for a large quilt, electric scissors are a great labor-saver. Cut the pieces from a single layer of cloth— if you try to cut more than one layer cloth may shift, and result in uneven pieces. Since the stitches will later be sewn along the pencil line, be careful that you do not erase the lines needed as a guide.

SEPARATE THE SHAPES: Separate the patches according to shape (some quilters prefer to keep separate groups for each patch). Sew a long thread through each pile of material, leaving the ends of the thread on the same side. This will hold the pile together and prevent scattering. Each piece can be slid off the thread as needed. Place the piles of material in a drawstring bag, box, or drawer near a comfortable chair with a good source of light nearby. You are now ready to sew.

PIECING A BLOCK: When all the pieces for the quilt are cut, sew them into patches as shown on dotted lines in Diagram 12.

Always after several seams have been sewn iron them flat before proceeding.

Repeat until there are forty blocks.

SEWING THE BLOCKS TOGETHER: Arrange these blocks into four rows of eight blocks each and sew together. Now sew the four rows together to form one large block.

Sew a 2½-inch white strip around the four sides of the block. Miter all corners. This means the corner must be sewn on a 90° diagonal from the inner corner to the outer. The border of the quilt should not be wider than ⅛ of the size of the finished quilt although it may be smaller.

WILD GOOSE CHASE BORDER, DIAGRAM 13: The border is Wild Goose Chase and the corners are Four Pointed Star. The corner star must be drawn to the exact size and the cardboard pieces cut as shown in Diagram 13. For a border that goes around

Diag. 13

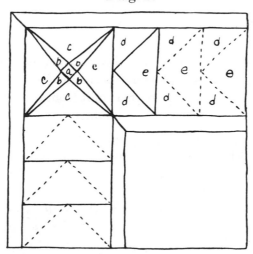

the whole quilt, there are four corner stars, each 4 x 4 inches square. To make these it will take four white one-inch square centers (a), sixteen red ¾-inch by 2½-inch triangles (b); and sixteen white 4 x 3-inch triangles (c). The Wild Goose Chase border for four sides of the quilt will take 80 green large triangles 4 x 2 inches (e); 160 white small triangles 2⅝ x 2 inches (d). These measurements do not include the seam allowance (Diagram 11).

SEWING CORNER BLOCKS: Sew the white square (a) to one of the long red triangles (b) then sew a white triangle (c) to the red triangle. Sew a second red triangle to the white triangle and the small white square. Then sew a white triangle to the red. Repeat until the last white triangle is sewn to the first triangle.

SEWING BORDER BLOCKS: Sew two white triangles (d) to a green triangle (e) to form an oblong 2 x 4 inches; sew several of these blocks together to form the border. Extreme care should be taken always to sew on the traced line so the strips and blocks will have straight sides. Now put the corner blocks and the border strips around four sides of the quilt and finish with the 2-inch white strip all around the outside, with all corners mitered. The finished quilt should look like Fig. 150.

STORING THE PATTERN: Always mark each cardboard shape with the name of the pattern and color of the material the piece should be cut from. These cardboard pieces should be very carefully kept together in an envelope marked with the pattern name. Should they be laid aside for a time before making the quilt or used later to make another quilt from the same pattern, the cardboard pieces will be kept intact.

EDGINGS, BORDERS AND STRIPS: Sometimes the bias tape which binds off a finished quilt is used as the border and the uninterrupted patterns do seem more modern and sophisticated; but for old-fashioned charm a border or edging of some contrasting fabric or design is often set into the quilt. A bound border requires that the blocks must cover the entire quilt top with an allowance made for a binding strip around the sides of the quilt. This binding strip is required to cover the raw edge left after the top, filler, and back have been quilted together. If the quilt is to be used as a spread, to cover the pillows also, the border may go around the four quilt sides. Otherwise the quilt will require a border on only three sides.

FILLING SPACES: When patterns are enlarged to form one central motif, it may be desirable to fill the corner spaces. When Lone Star is eight inches square, the blank corners are only two inches square, but when the patch is enlarged to eight feet those corners are two feet square. That is a considerable amount of blank space for a quilt top. Some of the motifs used to fill these spaces are: an appliquéd design that pleases the quilter; embroidery; the name of the quilter and date of starting and finishing the quilt; a quilted design similar to that used on the quilt in the frontispiece.

ENLARGING PIECES IN A QUILT PATCH: In some patterns two or more shapes in the same color adjoin each other. If these shapes combine into another shape which is easy to sew, they may be cut out as one piece. The Tulip Tree Leaves (Fig. 128) is an example.

LARGE BLOCKS: The enormous square Colonial quilts often used four squares of an intricate appliqué pattern similar to the one illustrated in Fig. 205. Each of these could measure three feet square or more. The border was correspondingly wide, sometimes exceeding a foot. This made a very rich-looking quilt which could be used effectively today with pieced patterns similar to Grandmother's Engagement Ring (Fig. 36), Ferris Wheel (Fig. 229), or Olive's Yellow Tulip (Fig. 63). Except for these cases quilts have a better appearance with smaller patches.

METHODS OF PUTTING BLOCKS TOGETHER: In the Duck Paddle Quilt the pieced quilt blocks were placed side by side. There are two other alternatives: lattice strips such as are used in the Shoo-fly quilt in Fig. 203; or alternate plain white blocks the same size as the pieced blocks, see Melon Patch Quilt (Fig. 2).

Making Appliquéd Quilts

Within limits, appliquéd quilts are made very much like pieced quilts. Color, size, and pattern must be decided upon first. The individual blocks must be made from ten to twenty-four inches square, rather than the eight to eighteen inches square of the pieced quilt patterns. The squares are larger because most appliqué patterns are more elaborate than piecework patterns.

Draw the pattern to the exact size on a piece of paper, then cut out the pieces and trace them on cardboard exactly like the piecework patterns. Where one piece overlaps another, extend the selvedge edge on the under piece to ½ inch. Then when the upper piece is tacked down the lower piece cannot pull loose.

All appliquéd patterns may be drawn using the steps illustrated in Diagram 14 as follows:

a. Draw a square the size of the finished appliqué design desired.

b. Draw lines as shown on Diagram 14A.

Diag. 14A　　　　　　　　　　　　　Diag. 14B

c. If the design has concentric circles, place them over the lines as shown in Diagram 14B.

d. Use the lines and circles as guides, draw in the pattern outlines. (Diagram 14C).

e. Cut out the paper pattern and then trace these patterns on cardboard.

Appliquéd patterns are sewn on the right side which indicates that the traced lines must also be on the right side of the cloth. Proceed as follows with the cloth on the cutting table:

a. Draw the patterns, leaving ¼-inch selvedge on all sides except for the pieces that fit under other pieces. Make these pieces ½-inch at the place where they are covered.

b. After the pieces are cut out, slit the selvedge edge of each piece to the pencil line on all concave and convex curves. An exception is where the piece projects under another. These slits are required to allow the folded edges to curve instead of forming straight lines. The selvedge must be cut off from any sharp points as shown in Diagram 14D.

c. Turn back all selvedge edges on all pieces and baste them to save difficulties when the pieces are tacked down.

Diag. 14C   *Diag. 14D*

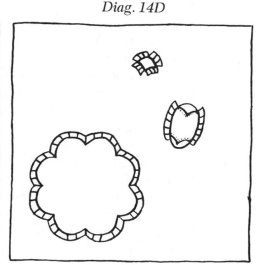

Remember that all pieces required for the whole quilt, including the squares for the background, must be cut out at once. Unbleached muslin makes a very good background material for quilts. It has the correct texture, is easy to sew, and large quantities are available very inexpensively. When unbleached muslin is washed, it becomes white and has a soft sheen. It also makes a very good background for other colors.

SEWING THE PIECES ON THE BACKGROUND

a. Measure the square and place a pin at the exact center.

b. Measure the large flower and place its exact center over the center of the square.

c. Pin the piece down and slide the leaf shapes into place under the edges and then pin them in place.

d. Sew the piece to be appliquéd in place using a very fine blind stitch. A number 60 or 70 thread of the same color as the appliquéd piece should be used.

e. Repeat for the other two flower shapes.

f. Care should be taken that the three pieces have the petal indentations lined up with the corners of the background piece (see Fig. 130).

g. Sew the leaf shapes in place and aligned with the indentations.

h. Place and overlap the buds on the ends of the leaf shapes.

i. Hem down the buds.

j. Sew the blocks together. The top is ready for the border.

If the background is to be made from a single sheet of muslin instead of square blocks, the measurements must be very exact. The corners of the patches must be measured off and marked. Mark the center of each piece with a pin. Take care that the patches are perfectly aligned vertically and horizontally on the back piece.

If the chosen pattern has embroidery for stems, or other lines too fine for appliquéd work, for example the Whig Rose (Fig. 369), then this embroidery should be done after all the pieces are sewn down. Mexican Rose (Fig. 129) shows an appliquéd pattern drawn by using only the straight lines and no concentric circles. The Double Tulip (Fig. 132) shows a patch that is half pieced and half appliquéd. In this case it is better to draw the two patterns as shown then work the pieced half, and finally add the appliqué (Diagrams 15 and 16). Framed Roses (Fig. 131) is the same type of half pieced, half appliquéd pattern except the pieced part of the patch forms a frame for the appliqué.

The border is put on last. If the pattern is a simple one, as the example is, an elaborate pattern may be used for the border, as Figs. 137, 138, 139 or 141. If, however, the pattern is as elaborate as Fig. 253, then Figs. 134 through 136 or 140 would be pretty.

As in pieced designs, some quilts do not need borders and look very nice with the edges simply bound off after quilting. Framed Roses (Fig. 131) is one of these.

When the quilt top is finished, the next step is the quilting. If you want to try quilting the top yourself, Chapter 6 will be of assistance. If you do not wish to do your own quilting, many ladies' church groups earn extra money by quilting. In Pennsylvania and North Carolina and other places there are women who quilt for extra money. They may be found by contacting the State Chamber of Commerce.

McCall's Needlework Magazine has been carrying ads for commercial quilting. These are for machine sewing and are comparatively reasonable.

Diag. 15

Diag. 16

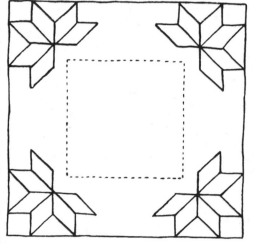
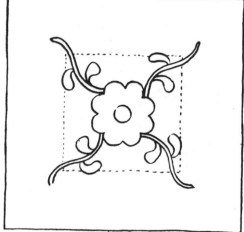

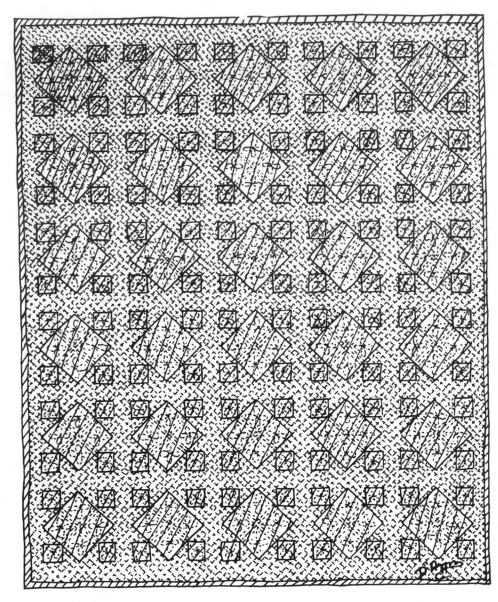

151. *A yellow on white nine-patch illustrating the quilter's rule of "simple pattern, elaborate quilting." (Mrs. Sara Nolph, owner.)*

VI

QUILTING

In Chapter V the making of a quilt top was discussed. This chapter deals with the method of stitching together the three layers that compose the quilt—the top, batting and the backing. Usually this stitching is ornamental and adds much to the beauty of the finished quilt.

This chapter will limit the study of quilts to the idea conveyed by one quilt definition:

"A quilt is not a quilt until it is quilted."

Since the warmth, strength, beauty, and value of a quilt depends upon its quilting as well as the quality of the sewing, a few rules should be observed.

Quilt Fillers

The amount of quilting will depend upon the filler; the looser the filler the greater the probability of its bunching together and causing damage to the quilt when washed. Cotton batting is the worst offender. Some cotton batts on the market are loosely prequilted, and bedcovers using the prequilted batts need not be quilted as closely as the loose cotton batts. A cotton sheet blanket on the other hand is woven, so a quilt using this type may be tied.

Two sizes of cotton batts are sold in the stores. One is a small size for crib quilts, the other is the larger size for adult quilts. The cotton must be the white long-fibered, well-bleached cotton and not the coarse, brown batts used by upholsterers.

Fillers may be any one of a number of materials. They may be either cotton batts previously mentioned, wool fleece, nylon, orlon, or any of the new fibers in fleece form.

A modern material called polyurethane foam has recently been put on the market in quilt-size batts. This material has the added advantage of retaining its body through use and repeated washings. This synthetic material cannot mat. Down (goose feathers), old blankets or flannel are some of the other types of filler. These are seldom used today; however, they are serviceable. In the past, tree bark, animal skins such as chamois, hair, leaves, moss, paper, strings, rags, game bird feathers, and many other unusual materials have been used as quilt fillers when the more conventional fillers were unavailable. Quilts have been dated by the newspapers, love letters, political papers, and diary pages found inside them. Old clothing, sweaters, stockings, worn out quilts and even paper money have provided warmth for many persons. "Waste not, want not," was the motto of most American quilters in the past.

Quilt Backing

The backing is usually a piece of muslin or other firm, inexpensive cloth. Natural, undyed homespun was used for a long time after machine-made cloth was used for the tops. Today, ordinary unbleached muslin, available at a nominal price, is the usual quilt backing.

Quilting Frames

Quilt top, filling, and backing must be put into a quilting frame. The way in which a quilt is assembled will depend upon the type of quilting frame. The oldest type frame is the easiest to work on, and allows the quilter to do her best sewing. Two pieces of 1 x 2-inch board the length of the quilt top plus 12 inches, are used for the front and back of the frame. These two pieces of wood are wrapped with three or four thickness of unbleached muslin and the side edges of the quilt are sewn to this. The side pieces of this frame are made of 1 x 2-inch boards and have a length equal to the width of the quilt plus 12 inches. These four boards are held together by "C" clamps which are available in any hardware store. The longer boards are placed over the shorter ones and a 4-inch overhang of each board is left at each corner. When the frame is assembled and the four clamps are tightened, the frame is placed over the backs of four wooden chairs. The best chairs for this purpose are the ladder back chairs or chairs having knobs or projections above the top slat of the backrest.

The biggest obstacle to this type of frame is the room it requires when assembled. It requires a large infrequently used room since the frame should be left in place until the quilt is finished. If the room is needed while the quilt frame is in place, the frame can be removed from the chairs and placed against one of the walls. The shorter side boards may be unclamped and the quilt rolled around the longer boards without unfastening it. Then the bundle can be placed in a closet. When the quilt frame is reassembled it must be put back with exactly the same tension on the quilt as when it was first erected.

Several needlework catalogs and department stores offer a moderately-priced table quilting frame, including directions for placing a quilt in it. There are also oval lap frames available, but these are not always satisfactory because the quilt having little tension may wrinkle as it is being sewn.

Assembling the Quilt on a Frame

1. Sew strips of unbleached muslin together for the backing. It must be the size and shape of the quilt top plus four inches on each of the four sides. Then sew one side of the muslin to the muslin wrapped around one of the longer pieces of the frame, with the raw edges of the seams up. Sew the opposite side of the muslin to the other pole of the frame. The muslin is pulled tight as it is being sewn, and the clamps are tightened to hold the muslin very taut.

2. Unfold the cotton batt with utmost care to prevent tearing holes in it. Lay it on the muslin. It will be too small at first but by sliding one hand under the cotton and lifting it at the same time, it can be gently stretched. It is easy to thin the cotton enough to fit the muslin. The cotton must not be pulled by the edges as large holes will be torn in it and these are never satisfactorily closed. The thinner the cotton, the neater and smaller the quilting stitches that can be made.

3. When the cotton is quite smooth and even, spread the quilt top over all and baste it to the backing around all four sides. If the backing and sides are not taut, loosen the "C" clamps on the two corners on the same side of the frame and pull the quilt tight. Then tighten the "C" clamps to hold the frame in that position. Perhaps it will be easier if two people do this tightening.

The Quilting Pattern

The quilting pattern depends on the quilt top pattern. Almost from the beginning American quilters have observed the convention of "a fancy quilting pattern for a plain quilt top and a simple outline or overall quilting pattern for a fancy top." Fancy patterns are those that must be traced from a pattern or drawn free-hand while the simpler patterns are those that can be drawn by tracing around a tea cup or along a ruler. The simplest quilting pattern of all is outline quilting where a line of running stitches is placed one fourth of an inch inside the seam line of a pieced square or appliquéd patch which causes the pattern of the quilt top to appear in the quilting stitches on the backing. Quilting the outline of the patterns in both piecework and appliquéd quilts is done on nearly half of the quilts made today. On an all-white quilt, or any quilt made with a simple piece of material as the quilt top, the quilting may be as ornate and fancy as the quilter has the skill to achieve.

SELECTING THE PATTERNS: Figs. 152 through 201 show a small fraction of the patterns that have been used for quilting. Figs.

152. *Double Lines (1848)*   153. *Diamonds (1808)*   154. *Shells (1860)*   155. *Circles*   156. *Basket Weave*   157. *Feathered Oval*   158. *Corner*   159. *Square*   160. *Single Feathered Wreath*   161. *Double Feathered Wreath*   162. *Feathered Cross*   163. *Feather Wreath*

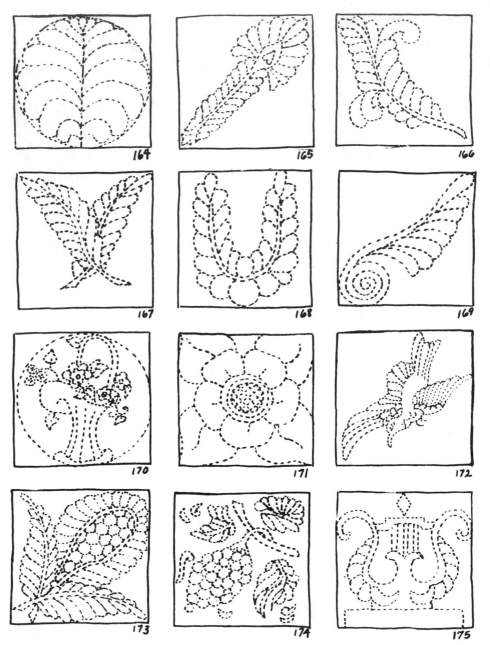

164. *Feather Circle*   165. *Feather Fan*   166. *Feather Plume*   167. *Crossed Feathers* (1865)   168. *Spray*   169. *Quill*   170. *Flower Basket*   171. *Wild Rose* 172. *Flying Bird*   173. *Feathered Pineapple*   174. *Grape*   175. *Harp*

152 through 157 show some patterns that may be used with medallions by leaving blank spaces in the pattern and filling these with one of the medallions on the following pages. Fig. 153 is especially effective when used in this manner. An appliqué or piecework pattern may be outlined and the blank spaces filled with the designs from Figs. 157 through 187. Figs. 160 through 169 show variations in the Princess' Feather designs. These Feather designs are very flexible and can be worked into almost any shape. They are just as effective in the simpler designs as the more complex ones. Figs. 176 through 187 give a few of the interesting medallion designs. Also shown are some of the many odd designs that quilters have adapted to their own purposes, such as flower motifs, etc.

Figs. 188 through 199 show a few ways to quilt a border. Notice Fig. 194 does not have a corner. If this one is used on a quilt, a corner must be worked out. On older quilts the borders of both the pieced top and the quilting were usually different for each of the four corners. The border was begun in one corner and worked out to fit into the next corner as the quilter sewed. The quilting for the corners was not thought out in advance. Modern thought dictates that this hit-or-miss system is not satisfactory. The border must be planned before the quilting or piecing is begun. The individual elements of the border must be measured first and fitted mathematically into the size of the quilt.

Also shown are many different-shaped fill-ins. These can be used in different ways, but usually fill in odd-shaped openings left when the pattern of the quilt top is quilted in outline. The last two figures of this series of designs, Figs. 200 and 201, are centers for all-white quilts. As such they should be expanded to two feet by four feet and three feet by four feet.

The one thing to remember when planning a quilting pattern is not to leave a space wider than three inches square; do so only when a space of that width is unavoidable. The tighter a quilt is quilted the stronger it will be and the longer it will wear.

PUTTING THE PATTERN ON CLOTH: The quilt tops that are quilted

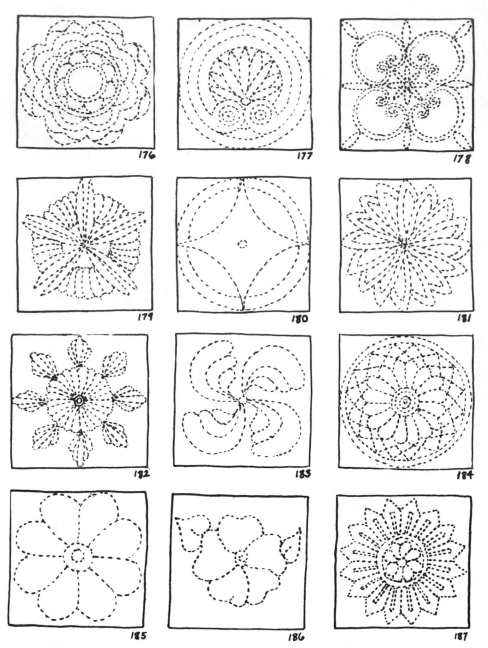

176. *Rose (1848)*   177. *Water Lily*   178-181. *Names unknown*   182. *Chrysan-*
themum   183. *Starfish*   184. *Daisy*   185. *Daisy*   186. *Flower*   187. *Flower*

in outline around the quilt pieces, or that are quilted in a simple overall design, are best drawn on the top. It has been found,
however, that more intricate designs can be drawn on the
white muslin backing, and quilted on that side. This does away
with errors caused by distracting effects from the pieced pattern. When quilting the top, remember to add a date and the
name of the quilter. This will be of particular interest to future
owners of the quilt.

There are many ways to put the pattern on the cloth. Experiment to find the easiest way for you. If you can draw free-
hand, draw the pattern on the muslin with a pencil and ruler.
For those less gifted, paper patterns are obtainable. These patterns have perforations that let through powder that marks the
pattern on the quilt. For simpler patterns as in Figs. 152 and 153
a yardstick is about the correct width, although the thin lines
on Fig. 152 should not be more than one-half inch in breadth.
For patterns of small circles, a teacup may be traced around.
For the larger circles, saucers, or plates may be used. A cup
or saucer is about the correct size for the pattern in Fig. 154,
while a plate may be used for Fig. 155. The pattern in Fig. 154
was adapted long ago from a New England pattern called
Clamshell (Fig. 107). This quilting pattern was thought so
pretty that it was used on quilts with other patches as well.

Homemade cardboard patterns can be used to outline a pattern; the connecting lines can then be drawn in.

Use a marker that can be washed out easily or one that will
not soil the pattern. Otherwise it will be difficult to follow when
sewing. With pencil or marking powder, the marks must not
be made too dark or too broad.

A popular way of marking a quilt is to rub a length of soft
cotton twine with blue chalk and fasten it securely and taut between the quilt's frame members. By lifting the string and let-
ting it snap back against the quilt, a blue chalk line is trans-
ferred to the white top.

When using the above methods, care must be taken to get
a sharp clear pattern without excess chalk deposits that must
be washed out. Care must also be taken when quilting not to
let the hands, arms, or clothing smear or erase the pattern be-

fore finishing the quilting. Properly marked, the quilt should not require laundering before it is used.

The whole pattern must be marked at one time when using a large frame. On smaller frames a small part of the quilt must be marked and sewn before another part can be started.

SEWING THE PATTERN: A small, straight, Number 10 needle is the most convenient size for quilting. With continued use the needle will develop a slight curvature which will improve it as a quilting needle. When quilters did most of their sewing by hand, they would use their new needles for ordinary sewing and when the needle developed this curvature it was laid aside for use as a quilting needle.

A number 30 or 40 thread was formerly used when quilting; however, it was found that a fine thread sewn more evenly and closely (one inch or less) between stitched lines produced equivalent strength and neater appearance. Quilting evenly is easier if you make sure that all selvedge edges in the quilt top and backing are not more than one-quarter inch wide; also, there must be no lumps or holes in the cotton filler. The top and backing plus filler must be basted firmly all over the surface as well as around the edge when using a lap frame or when quilting without a frame. The more basting you do, the better the quilt will be held to prevent wrinkles. Both of these methods are possible but are not always satisfactory.

Quilting is done along one end of the quilt in a strip about one foot wide. The "C" clamps are then loosened and the quilt is rolled tightly around the stock and the clamps are retightened. Since the roll of quilt gets quite unwieldy when the quilt is about half finished, work may be done first on one side and then on the other side. In quilting bees several women would take places on alternate sides of a quilt and work toward the center.

Padded Work

Some quilting patterns have raised portions incorporated in the design. This type of pattern is called padded work and is

188. *Lazy Daisy Border*   189. *Twisted Rope Border*   190. *Woven Border No. 1*
191. *Woven Border No. 2*   192. *Circle Border*   193. *Floral Border*   194. *Feathered Border*   195. *Chain Border*   196. *Rose Border*   197. *Double Cable*
198. *Waved Feather Band (1808)*   199. *Swag*

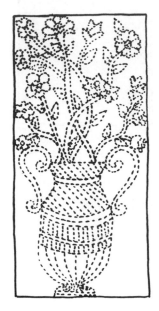

200. *Victorian Design for All-White Quilt*

201. *Modern Design for All-White Quilt*

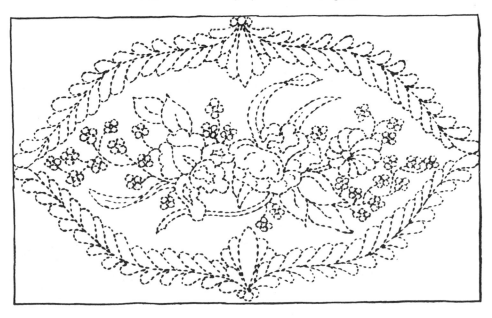

done by inserting a piece of thick string under the muslin for stems and thin scrolls. For flowers and other broad areas extra cotton is stuffed into place. The padded work is accomplished as follows:

a. Complete the quilting and outline all flowers, stems or other raised portions using close stitches.

b. Make an opening between the threads of muslin backing. A knitting needle is best for this purpose. Care must be taken to prevent breaking the muslin threads.

c. Enlarge the opening by a slight circular movement of the needle until the opening is slightly larger than the needle diameter.

d. Take pieces of string or a thin strip of cotton batting as padding, and using the same needle poke the padding into the opening until the space between the stitching is stuffed full.

e. Work the padding to the top of the design and work it straight with the fingers.

f. Close the opening in the muslin backing when the padding is completed. The separated muslin threads are gently worked in place with fingers. At the same time the muslin is twisted back and forth to make it lay smooth and uniform.

Trimming and Binding

When the quilt is finished and taken off the frame, it is trimmed and bound. A matching color of wide bias tape may be used, or one-inch strips may be cut on the bias from a piece of the material used in the quilt. If the backing is wide enough, the quilt top and filler may be trimmed and the backing brought forward and sewed in a hem around the quilt. Whichever is used, care must be taken to miter the corners for a neat appearance.

A sewing machine may be used to stitch the tape to the quilt top. Pin the tape on first and baste the miters in the corners to get them perfectly even. When the top side of the bias tape is sewn on, fold over the other side and baste it down. Now blind stitch the back of the tape with stitches small enough to be unnoticeable.

202. *Navy blue and white have always been the traditional colors for the Jacob's Ladder quilt. The pattern is good for a boy's room.*

Washing Quilts

When washing a quilt set the machine for warm water, never hot water. If the machine has a setting for fragile fabrics, it should be used in preference to a heavier setting. Quilts are usually too heavy when wet to allow for hand washing. Never wring the water out of a quilt or twist it unduly—such treatment will break the stitches and weaken the quilt.

Use mild soap or detergent. Dry it in a dryer, if possible, since a dryer fluffs the cotton filler and will make the quilting look better. Drying a quilt on the line is also possible, however, and when this is necessary the quilt should be pinned along two sides to two different lines. This will prevent the quilt's weight from pulling out or breaking the threads. Never iron a quilt as the quilting will not stand out, thus spoiling the effectiveness of the whole quilt.

Unless the quilt is made of wool, mothballs or other preservatives are not required; merely store the quilt like any other good linen. The old custom of putting lavender with the linens is a good one because the quilts will have a pleasing odor when they are put on the bed.

A quilt should be washed approximately every five years when it is in storage to prevent unnecessary yellowing of the fabric. When a quilt is in use it should be washed only often enough to prevent it from becoming deeply soiled but not oftener than twice a year. A quilt that has been given moderate care should last through fifty years of use. Many quilts in museums are of course much older than fifty years. These show their signs of wear with pride.

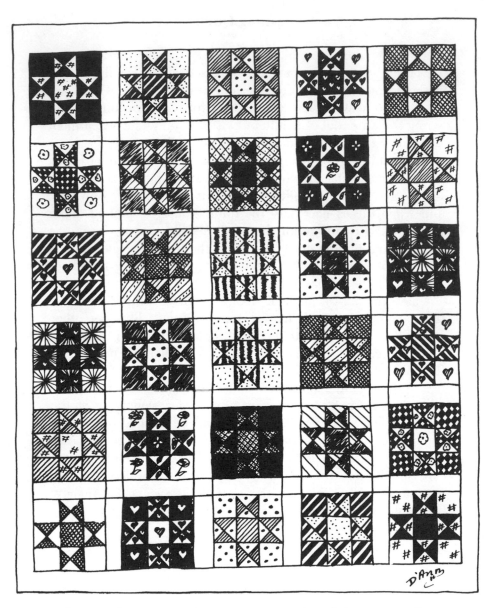

203. The Shoo-fly pattern made up as a scrap quilt with lattice strips between the blocks is a neat and pretty way to use scraps from the cutting table.

VII

SEWING A QUILT
BY MACHINE

Many women would as lief try to get along without a range or vacuum cleaner as to try to keep house without their sewing machines. This chapter is included for these women.

Anyone with patience and determination can hand-sew a quilt, but making a quilt by machine is quite a different matter. To obtain the best instructions possible, I consulted several well-qualified seamstresses. The information in this chapter came from a lady who has been teaching machine sewing for a sewing machine company for twenty years. Even though this woman is an expert and used one of the latest model machines, she had difficulty with certain problems. These difficulties are indicated in the following text.

Piecing a Quilt by Machine

Some women have always used their sewing machines for piecing quilts, but discretion in choosing the pattern is necessary. A pattern with straight-sided pieces that are larger than three inches across are more easily machine-sewn than curved pieces or pieces smaller than three inches across.

A straight-sided piece is easier to sew than a curved piece. By hand the two curves may be eased into one another, but by machine, this is not easily done. An expert seamstress who is capable of putting in a notched, tailored collar without diffi-

culty, would be able to piece patterns with curved pieces by
following these steps:

1. On paper, draw the pattern to the exact size.

a. Use the directions in Chapter V and cut out one piece of
each different size or shape for use as a stencil.

b. Place the paper stencil on a piece of heavy cardboard and
draw a line around it.

c. By measuring very carefully, draw another line exactly ¼
inch larger, all around.

d. Cut the pattern on the outside line (as drawn in step c).

e. Using very sharp scissors, cut out the middle part on the first
line drawn.

f. With the cardboard pattern placed on the wrong side of the
fabric, trace a line around edges of it.

g. Cut the cloth on the outside line and sew it together on the
inside line.

2. Do not cut the points off the seam allowances, as in hand
sewing. Cut the excess material from the wrong side of the
points after the seam is finished, if required.

3. When sewing curves, clip the seam allowances on the
concave curves as shown on shape 1 in the diagram. Clip the
seam allowances ¼ inch apart on tight curves and up to ½ inch
apart on slight curves. Place the concave curve atop the convex
curve to sew. Try to exactly match the two pencil lines.

4. Fold the two pieces in half and press a fold with the fingers in the middle of each piece and at the lines to be sewn.

a. Place the two creases together.

b. Carefully move the pieces to begin sewing in one corner.

5. Set the machine pressure at the normal level and use the
tightest stitch (18 to 20 stitches per inch, if possible). This will
prevent the stitches from raveling after clipping without tying
a knot at each corner.

6. Use the regular foot on the machine for piecing. There
should be a ¼-inch flange on the right side. This will be a useful guide when sewing a seam allowance which must be exactly
¼ inches wide.

7. Lay out the pieces for a patch in the exact order they
should go when sewn onto a patch. This will avoid confusion

over the pattern, since machine sewing is much faster than hand sewing.

8. Care should be taken when sewing the pieces together that all of the seam allowances will be on the wrong side of the patch when finished. With the stitches set so small the fabric will tear before the stitches can be removed if an error is made.

9. Use new thread. Older thread may be dry-rotted.

10. Iron the seam allowance flat after every three or four seams.

By using care and being exact at every step of the process, the quilt pieced by machine should be as beautiful as any hand-sewn quilt.

To repeat: Piecing curved patterns on a machine is not recommended until you are familiar with every phase of machine sewing and have made several quilts using patterns without curves.

Appliqué by Machine

Appliquéing by machine may be done on many items other than quilts. The more automatic the sewing machine, the fancier the appliquéd work that may be done. To make sure that you can use the machine to its fullest extent and can make use of all its automatic features, take the lessons offered by the company when buying a new model machine. The new automatic machines will give wonderful results to an operator who knows the machine, its capabilities and its limitations.

HERE ARE THE STEPS:

1. Draw the appliqué pattern to scale on paper and then on cardboard as directed in Chapter V. Draw the pattern on the right side of the material and leave a seam allowance of ¼ inch on each side. Do not clip the seam allowance as is done for hand sewing.

2. Set the foot pressure at its lightest weight, short of setting for darning which gives no pressure at all.

3. Set the stitch length at its shortest point, at least 20 stitches per inch.

4. Use the foot part of the quilting foot without its guide, or the special short foot, although the latter does not allow the machine as much flexibility for turning short corners.

5. Stitch each piece to the background along the sewing line. Sew very slowly, and hold each piece in place firmly with the left hand. With the right hand, hold a pair of sharp-nosed scissors or a nail file and ease the material under the foot without allowing it to stretch or buckle.

6. Cut off the seam allowance very close to the line of stitches without cutting the stitches.

7. Cover the raw edge of the material with a fancy stitch. Two of the fancy stitches made on an automatic machine that are especially suitable for appliquéing are the zig-zag stitch and the buttonhole stitch. The latter is sometimes called the comb stitch.

THE ZIG-ZAG STITCH: Set the machine for its finest stitch (20 per inch) and with the pressure set very light, use the special short foot. This foot has a square opening instead of the usual slot and will permit the needle to move back and forth. The width of the stitch can be regulated. Usually this is accomplished by a lever on a gage. Experiment with various stitch widths and spare pieces of cloth before beginning to appliqué. Use the stitch width best suited to cover the seam. It may be better to vary the stitch width to suit the size of patch.

Diagram 17 shows a leaf completely worked in zig-zag stitch, while in Diagram 18 only the center of the flower is zig-zag. The zig-zag stitch at 20 stitches per inch resembles the satin stitch. The vein of the leaf was also made with the zig-zag stitch in the following manner: Starting at the base of the flower and with the lever set for a wide stitch, make several stitches. Slide the lever to the next smaller setting and make several more stitches. Continue until the machine has made one or two straight stitches for the point of the vein. It may be well to practice this stitch before applying it to an appliquéd piece.

THE BUTTONHOLE STITCH: In Diagram 18 the outline stitch is

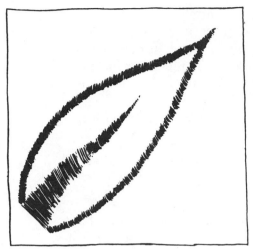

Diag. 17   Diag. 18

shown at A. The buttonhole stitch, sewn at 20 stitches per inch is shown at B. A third fancy stitch is shown at C. This third stitch is pretty but does not cover the edge as well as the buttonhole stitch. It may be well to try other stitches on another piece of cloth to find a stitch that will cover the edges of appliquéd patches as well as those mentioned above. The stitch at 4 shows the buttonhole stitch worked at less than 20 stitches per inch. It will be noticed that this latter does not satisfactorily cover the raw edge on the patch.

On nonautomatic machines, appliquéing may be done by setting the pressure very light and stitching at twenty stitches per inch. To cover the raw edges, hand embroidery may also be used.

Machine Appliqué for Small Articles

1. Lay out the backing, cut to size and shape as shown in Chapter VI.

2. Cover the backing with a thin layer of quilting cotton and lay the appliqué background over this.

3. Baste the three layers together firmly.

4. Pin the appliqué pieces in place and sew through the three layers, thus appliquéing and quilting in one operation.

If appliquéd pieces are not close enough together for holding the cotton well, a quilting design may be added between the appliqué.

The edges of appliquéd patches may be covered with fancy stitching, as usual.

Quilting by Machine

Quilting may be done on any machine from the newest automatic to the oldest treadle by following a few simple rules.

1. Lay out the backing and spread the quilting cotton thinly over it. Spread the top over the cotton and pin the three layers together.

2. Baste the three layers together firmly, beginning in the middle and sewing in an outward spiral. A large clear area of the floor or a table larger than the quilt is the best place to do this work. Care should be taken not to move the quilt until it is entirely basted.

3. Fold the basted quilt diagonally from corner to corner.

4. Iron the creases at 1. and 2. into the fabric (Diagram 19).

5. Set the stitch indicator on your machine for from 12 to 15 stitches per inch, and set the pressure foot of the machine to a little lighter than normal. Use the quilting foot with a guide. This foot is rounded to turn up at the end. This allows it to rest lightly on the quilt without matting the cotton filler.

DIAMOND PATTERN: Sew along the previously ironed-in creases from corner to corner. This will anchor the corners to a 45-degree angle. Set the guide on the quilting foot to the width needed for the space between the sewn lines. These lines are to be maintained for the whole quilt. Sew one line along each side of line 1; one line in one direction, the second line in the reverse direction. Repeat for line 2. There are 6 lines sewn on the quilt as shown in Diagram 19. Sew the two lines, 7 and 8, to the right of line 1 and from side a. to side b. Starting from

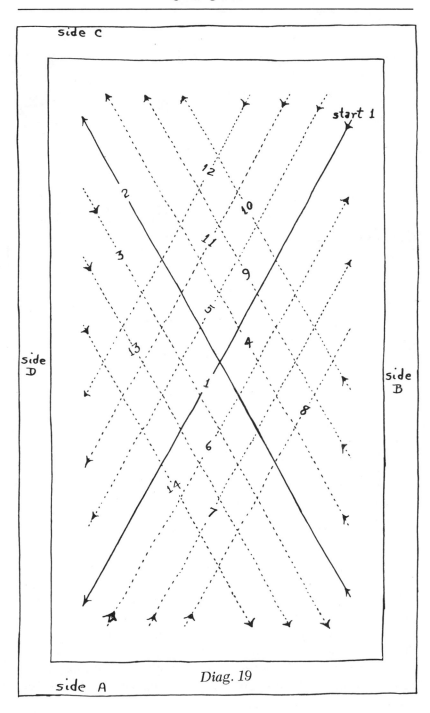

side C

side
D

side
B

side A

Diag. 19

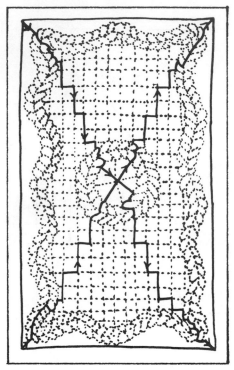

Diag. 20A

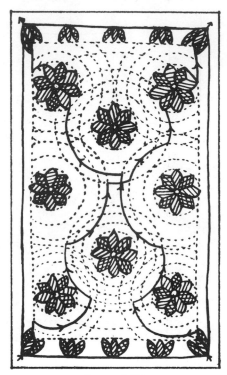

Diag. 20B

side b., sew lines 9 and 10 and terminate the lines at side c. Starting at side c., sew lines 11 and 12 toward side d. Continue sewing two lines successively from each side of the quilt until the entire pattern is completed.

FOR FANCIER PATTERNS: The pattern is first drawn on the backing as directed in Chapter VI and is completed as follows:

Sew the quilt to the backing from corner to corner as near the creases as the pattern permits (Diagrams 20A and 20B). Set the pressure on the machine to darning (zero pressure). For older model machines, the nut is removed from the foot bar. This removal will not harm the machine. Having removed the pressure on the foot, the material being sewn may be moved freely in any direction needed to follow even the most intricate pattern. Care must be taken to keep the length of the stitches somewhat even as the machine cannot regulate its own stitches without pressure. Practice on a piece of spare material before working on the quilt itself.

After sewing the quilt from corner to corner on the pattern, sew the pattern for two or three inches on either side of the first lines. Then in the same manner as the diamond pattern, continue turning the quilt and sewing two or three-inch widths of the pattern until the quilt is completed.

The above suggestions may seem to over-emphasize details and be a fussy way to quilt; but by starting in the middle of the quilt, puckers can be eased ahead of the sewing as progress is made all the way to the edges. This will ensure a smooth quilt. Also, by working small widths and frequently turning the quilt, the strain and stretching are equalized over all portions of the quilt and will result in a square when completed. These problems are usually resolved by the frame when quilting by hand.

OUTLINE QUILTING: Place the quilt top uppermost, set the machine for very light pressure and sew a line of stitches from corner to corner and as near the crease as the quilt pattern will permit. Two methods may be used. 1. Quilting in a line but leaving a ¼-inch gap at each seam by lifting the foot and leaving a loose loop of thread. These threads may be cut and knotted later. This method requires more time and is more difficult to accomplish. However, it does give one the same impression as a hand-quilted outline pattern. 2. The pattern is sewn from side to side across the pattern and ¼ inch from the seam which it parallels without leaving spaces at the seams crossed.

As previously mentioned, new thread should be used when quilting by either machine or by hand to ensure strength and longer life.

204. *This pictorial quilt made by the author in 1960 is based on the crazy-quilt method. The background was filled in, then the clown and his balloons were appliquéd on top. His shoes, hat brim and balloons are stuffed. The pompons and balloon strings are made of cotton yarn.*

VIII

PERSONALIZING

YOUR QUILT

There are many sources of ideas for quilt patterns. In addition to the patterns described in this or other books, the quilter has freedom in selecting color combinations, varying the pieces, and changing the scale and proportion of all the elements.

Inspiration from Familiar Scenes

Quilt patterns have been developed from sketches of flower sprays. A personal touch may be added to the pattern by selecting sprays from one's own garden. A Basket quilt similar to Fig. 113 originated by filling the basket with fruit, flowers, birds, etc., as seen from the quilter's window. A quilter living on tiny Nantucket Island made a quilt with appliquéd pictures of the houses and public buildings of the town as she remembered it from childhood; lattice strips were used between the blocks to represent the streets. A wounded soldier recovering from the Civil War made a quilt of rows of soldiers in many kinds of uniforms. Another man in the Midwest won prizes in many county fairs for his fine quilts. Each quilt was a representation of a famous biblical painting, done in the manner of a stained glass window. These quilts had thousands of carefully selected pieces in hundreds of tints and shades of colors.

One pattern for an appliquéd quilt was obtained from a clock face, the Seth Thomas Rose (Fig. 250). Seth Thomas

205. *The Triple Tulip. Four appliquéd squares and a border make up the top of this quilt reproduction. The original was made in the 1930s, but the idea of using four squares for a top is a colonial one. With the squares as much as three feet in width and length very elaborate patterns can be used. (Mrs. Sara Nolph, owner.)*

carved wooden clocks in a small town in New England. In the summer he loaded his clocks into a peddler's cart and ranged far and wide over the early American states. The clocks were sold to farmers and merchants. Seth Thomas' clocks were very popular because of the ease with which they could be repaired. The wooden works facilitated such repairs by those possessing average skill in the use of tools. These clocks were usually decorated with painted flowers, and one of these flower designs was used in the pattern referred to above.

One of the loveliest quilts brought to the author's attention was a basic Double Irish Chain similar to Fig. 121. The quilt was in dainty colors and well made, and used bouquets of different flowers embroidered into the blank spaces.

Rearranging the Basic Elements

Very simple patches can, by rearrangement, be made into many attractive patches. Figs. 206-217 show twelve different patterns, the most famous of which is Drunkard's Path (Fig. 206). All but one of these patterns are made by simply rear-

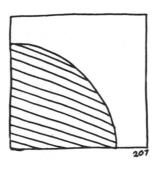

206. *Drunkard's Path*   207. *Basic Patch*   208. *Rocky Road to Dublin*

ranging the basic patch (Fig. 207). The one exception Steeple Chase (Fig. 214) has two semi-circles cut from the basic patch instead of just one. Figs. 218 through 229 show several four-patch designs and Figs. 230 through 241 show nine-patch designs. These were all developed by slight changes of the original pattern.

Appliquéd flowers are simplified versions of flowers seen growing in nature. Figs. 242-277 are of roses and tulips. Many additional patterns may be developed by using the basic pattern and changing the buds, leaves, etc. from pattern to pattern. Different parts of the borders may be recombined in various ways or use may be made of the basic idea from one of the floral borders shown.

209. *Fool's Puzzle*   210. *Wonder of the World*   211. *Falling Timbers*
212. *Around the World*   213. *Rob Peter to Pay Paul*   214. *Steeple Chase*

215. *Mill Wheel*   216. *Love Ring*   217. *Robbing Peter to Pay Paul*

Inspiration from the Kitchen

Dish decorations were often copied in quilt patterns. Both the painted and transfer prints were copied. The author has seen patterns on china very similar to the Rose (Fig. 259), Conventional Tulip (Fig. 270), and Maud Hare's Flower Garden (Fig. 280). Dishes and vases gave their forms to many patterns. There are Tulips in a Bowl (Fig. 263), and Grandmother's Tulips (Fig. 264). These are all appliquéd designs. A piecework design which suggests glass, cut glass, or sandwich glass dishes is The Pickle Dish (Fig. 287).

Nostalgic Quilts

During the 1890s and into the 1930s, patterns became very graphic. There was a nostalgic wish for things to be as they had been. Changes were coming too rapidly for most people and they seemed to want their quilts to picture an older, pleasanter time. This was when Crazy Quilts reached the heights of extravagance and many were made to record family histories. One, for example, has pieces gathered from many members of a very large family. Each piece is embroidered with name, birth date, death date (when needed), and an appropriate sentiment of the donor. Incorporated into this quilt are such things

218. *Four-Patch* 219. *Four-Patch* 220. *Coffin Star* 221. *Robbing Peter to Pay Paul* 222. *Pinwheel* 223. *Cross and Crown* 224. *Nelson's Victory* 225. *Pinwheel* 226. *Arkansas Traveler* 227. *Sunflower Star* 228. *Mariner's Compass* 229. *Ferris Wheel*

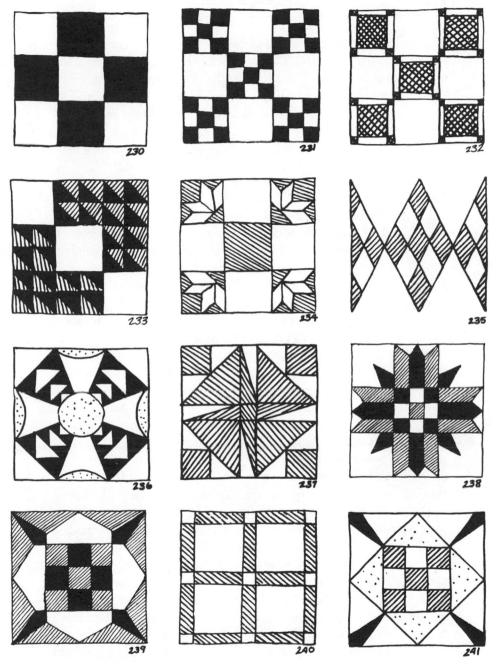

230. Nine-Patch 231. Double Nine-Patch 232. Puss in the Corner 233. Winged
Square 234. Mexican Star 235. Nine-Patch Diamond 236. Dusty Miller
237. Crazy Ann 238. Alice's Favorite 239. Chain of Diamonds 240. Nine-
Patch 241. Nine-Patch Star

as a man's hat band, a leather bow tie, a piece of corset cover complete with lace, etc. This too, was the era of quilts made with blocks similar to The Little Red School House (Fig. 290), The Town Pump (Fig. 291), Sunbonnet Sue (Fig. 292), The Colonial Lady (Fig. 293), Butterflies (Fig. 294), and, most ridiculous of all, Horseshoes (Fig. 295).

Trees

Trees have been very popular since the earliest Colonial days. The first flags were all made by quilters and it was no coincidence that a great many of the flags used by American soldiers were Pine Tree Flags. The Pine Tree meant steadfastness and loyalty and was a favorite New England quilting motif. There are two Pine Trees illustrated (Figs. 42 and 115). Other trees were Tree Everlasting (Fig. 297), and Tree of Temptation (Fig. 298). The Tree of Temptation is actually a religious pattern even though it does not look like one. The colors are red, green, and white with brown trunk. The red squares represent the apples that tempted Adam and Eve. As can be seen, the boughs bend low so the apples may be easily reached.

Leaves too form many of the patterns. The oldest pattern in this group is called Palm Leaves, Hosannah! (Fig. 299). This pattern was known in early New England and has appeared all over the United States. It can be used as shown in the illustration, or one-fourth of the square can be combined with one of the other religious patterns to be used in a checker-board pattern. A row of one-fourth of this pattern would also make a lovely border for a religious quilt when joined either to form a diamond-shaped or a straight border. Leaves are used on almost all of the flower appliqués. These were sometimes just pointed ovals or other simple leaf shapes. Occasionally leaf shapes were selected from maple, oak, poplar, or other trees for use as patterns. They give a lovely effect when appliquéd to the top among the appliquéd flowers. Leaves were used for pieced designs like the Tulip Tree Leaf (Fig. 128). Two other patterns illustrated are Maple Leaf (Fig. 300) and Buckeye Leaf (Fig. 303).

242. *Whig Rose* 243. *Rose of Sharon* 244. *Mexican Rose* 245. *Rose of Sharon* 246. *Conventional Rose* 247. *Old-Fashioned Rose* 248. *Rose* 249. *Rose of Sharon* 250. *Seth Thomas Rose* 251. *Pink Rose* 252. *Whig Rose* 253. *Elaborate Patch*

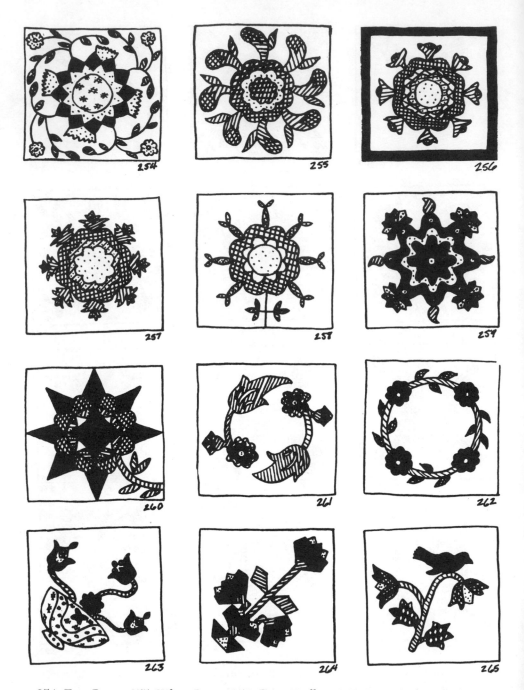

254. *Tea Rose* 255. *Whig Rose* 256. *Rose Trellis* 257. *Rose Bud* 258. *Rose Appliqué* 259. *Rose* 260. *Harrison's Rose (1880)* 261. *Wild Rose* 262. *Rose Wreath* 263. *Tulips in a Bowl* 264. *Grandmother's Tulip* 265. *Pennsylvania Dutch Design*

266. *Modernistic Tulip*   267. *Garden Tulip*   268. *Single Tulip*   269. *Tulip*
270. *Conventional Tulip*   271. *Trailing Tulips*   272. *Tulip Design*   273. *Grandma's Tulip*   274. *Conventional Tulips*   275. *Colonial Tulip*   276. *Conventional Tulip*   277. *Pomegranate*

278. *Bearded Iris* (1962)   279. *Thistles*   280. *Maud Hare's Flower Garden*
281. *Columbine* 282. *Snow on the Mountain* 283. *Triple Sunflower* 284. *Poinsettia* 285. *Magnolia Bud* 286. *Cornucopia* 287. *Pickle Dish* 288. *Ice Cream Bowl* 289. *Fish in the Dish*

290. *Little Red School House*   291. *Old Town Pump*   292. *Sunbonnet Sue*
293. *The Colonial Lady*   294. *Butterflies*   295. *Horseshoes*   296. *The Cross*
297. *Tree Everlasting* 298. *Tree of Temptation*   299. *Palm Leaves, Hosannah!*
300. *Maple Leaf* 301. *Maple Leaf*

Many patterns do not resemble the things they are supposed to represent. The Brown Goose (Fig. 71) is a typical example. Others in the category are, respectively: Flock of Geese, Chimney Swallows, Dove in the Window, Cats and Mice, Rose Bud, Flying Clouds, and Storm at Sea (Figs. 304 through 310). The latter design, however, does have a restless appearance. Oddly enough, many patterns are named for stars that do not resemble stars in the slightest degree. Five of these patterns are shown in Figs. 311 through 315, each of which has an intrinsic beauty but is definitely not a star.

Scrap Quilts

Scrap quilts were mentioned previously in this book but were not referenced to an illustration. Some beautiful ones which the reader may not have seen are Basket of Scraps (Fig. 316), Baby Aster (Fig. 89), Wedding Ring Bouquet (Fig. 317), and Ferris Wheel (Fig. 229). The latter two are favored by many quilters as having the greatest eye appeal.

Baby Quilts

Pieced-quilt designs small enough and yet not too intricate for baby quilts are rather rare. Springtime Blossoms (Fig. 318), also known as Hearts and Gizzards or Pierrot's Pom-Pom, makes an attractive baby quilt. A pattern which a friend made for my baby son and which I call Trey's Quilt (Fig. 319) was quilted in a flowered chintz. The chintz is printed in tiny yellow flowers with green leaves. A quilt which may be made for a crib or regular bed size is the Box Quilt (Fig. 320). This quilt is also called Baby Blocks. Attractive baby quilt designs and ones having equally appropriate names are the Baby Bunting (Fig. 321), Grandma's Red and White Quilt (Fig. 322) and Blue Birds for Happiness (Fig. 325).

Quilt patterns can be very similar and yet when the details of each pattern are examined they will be seen to be quite dif-

302: *Sweet Gum Leaf*   303. *State of Ohio*, also called *Buckeye Leaf*   304. *Flock of Geese*   305. *Chimney Swallows*   306. *Dove in the Window*   307. *Cats and Mice*   308. *Rose Bud*   309. *Flying Clouds*   310. *Storm at Sea*   311. *Nine-Patch Star*   312. *Morning Star*   313. *New Star*

314. *St. Louis*   315. *Star*   316. *Basket of Scraps*   317. *Wedding Ring Bouquet*
318. *Springtime Blossoms*   319. *Trey's Quilt*   320. *Pandora's Box*, also called
Box Quilt, and *Baby Blocks*   321. *Baby Bunting*   322. *Grandma's Red and White
Quilt*   323. *Sailboats*   324. *String of Beads*   325. *Blue Birds for Happiness*

ferent. There are four patterns derived from the Snowball (Figs. 328-331). Even when these patterns are placed close together, the differences are not always noticeable. The two patterns, Dresden Plate and Lazy Daisy (Figs. 332, 333), show what can happen when two or three quilters use the same cardboard pattern for quilts. The cardboard was drawn for the Dresden Plate, and was then traced for a second pattern. This second pattern was used for the Lazy Daisy. The Dresden Plate is a pieced quilt but the Daisy petals were sewn together and appliquéd onto the background.

Ideas from Ads

Quilt patterns can sometimes be found in newspaper ads. Writers of advertising text are fond of using little stylized designs to brighten up otherwise dull subjects. The two designs in Figs. 326 and 327 were used respectively in an advertisement of carpeting and one promoting National Diary Week. Both make excellent quilt patterns. In fact, the second appealed to me so much that when a baby quilt was needed for a new cousin in the family, I made one in this pattern and called it Ice-Cream Cone. At the time this quilt was made, I wanted a yellow flannel backing. Because of summer weather this material was not available in the stores, so a soft yellow blanket was used for the backing. It worked very well. Substitution of materials often gives surprisingly good results and helps to personalize the quilt.

Names on Quilts

Quilts may be personalized in a manner which will enhance their value and interest with age. This may be accomplished by embroidering the quilter's name and the date into the quilting design of a block or along the edge of the quilt. India ink may also be used for this purpose. This will preserve the memory of the quilter's name and date of the quilt. So many beautiful quilts are handed down in families where the quilter and the quilt's age are uncertain.

The three patterns (Figs. 335-337) are autograph patches. Even if autographed quilts are old-fashioned, it is still pleasant to have the names of friends on a quilt. After the patch has been made the friend's name may be written on the patch using India ink or a pencil. The pencil tracing will serve as a guide for embroidery. The patches are sewed to the quilt top after all available names have been obtained.

Patterns may be used as first observed or they may be enlarged, made smaller, changed slightly in color, or shape. Patterns may be pictorial to an advanced degree, or lack association with that which their names imply. They may be simple or they may be elaborate. There is no specific formula to be followed in order to create a quilting masterpiece.

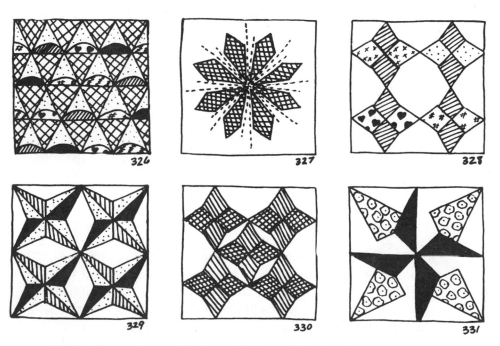

326. *Ice Cream Cone*   327. *Star*   328. *Snowball*   329. *Star*   330. *Pontiac Star*   331. *Blazing Star*

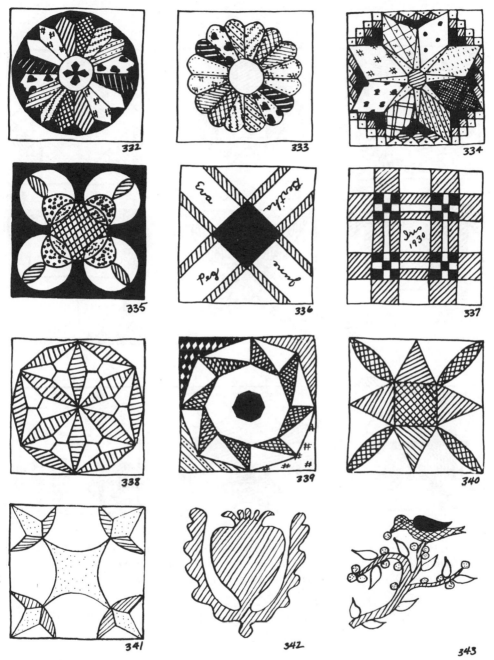

332. *Dresden Plate*   333. *Lazy Daisy*   334. *Shadow Star*   335. *Hero's Crown*
336. *Autograph Patch*   337. *Album Patch*   338. *Chained Star*   339. *Carnival Time*   340. *Morning Star*   341. *Wandering Foot*   342. *Pineapples*   343. *The Dove*

344. *Whirling Swastika* 345. *Delectable Mountains (center)* 346. *Delectable Mountains (outer patch)* 347. *The Rambler* 348. *Harlequin Star* 349. *Twisting Star* 350. *Rose Quilt* 351. *Friendship Knot* 352. *Autumn Leaf*

IX

QUILTING CUSTOMS AND
SUPERSTITIONS

Many things have affected quilt patterns down through the years. As a general trend, when the economic picture of the country was dark, geometric and simple patterns were popular. After a recession more elaborate patterns became the vogue, and when, as in 1830 and 1890, there was an era of sudden optimism and plenty, overblown and over-elaborate patterns were very popular, only to fall into disuse when a downward economic trend recurred.

Colors, too, have had many cycles in popularity, keeping pace with dress fashions because most quilts were made from dress scraps. It was long after the industrial revolution that cloth became more plentiful and a quilter could afford the extravagance of buying material just for quilt making.

The earliest quilts were made, of course, in the heavy, rather dark materials the colonists used for their clothing; maroons, browns, and dark greens being special favorites. The first cloth made in the colonies was crude, the dyeing was uncertain, and the results were often very unsatisfactory. The usual colors obtained from these dyes were orange, yellow, green, blue, and brown, especially a brown called "butternut." The dyemakers did not have sufficient skill to enable them to make a good, permanent red. This necessitated the importation of red cloth from England.

In a letter about Martha Washington, the writer mentions that most of the new clothing worn by Mrs. Washington and

353. *The Windmill was a utility pattern, easily cut out and quickly sewn together but not noted for its looks. Old utility quilts are hard to find as they did not receive the care given to the more elaborately patterned quilts.*

her servants was made at Mt. Vernon of cloth from their own looms, the one exception being the red cuffs and collars on the coachmen's uniforms. Because of her husband's status, Mrs. Washington had to maintain favorable appearances. Since her dye pot could not produce a satisfactory red, enough red cloth to meet their needs was imported.

This imported red cloth was used sparingly by any one fortunate enough to possess it. The unused pieces were carefully preserved and passed along for future generations' use. The author read of one red cloak owned by a Lord Mayor of London that was brought to this country by his son in the seventeenth century. It was worn well into the eighteenth century, and was then used for quilt patches until 1880 when the last remnant was used in a quilt by a descendant of the original Lord Mayor.

Around 1830 quilts made of red, green, and white became very popular, but it was not until 1880 when the cloth called turkey-red was imported from Germany that solid red and white quilts could be made (Fig. 354). Turkey-red was a good, permanent, non-fading red. Cloth made from American dyes ran and faded to pink within three washings. It took the First World War, when European imports were unobtainable, to start American dyemakers on the trail of a permanent red. They succeeded in finding several; but it was not until after the Second World War that permanent shades of red became available in cloth of all price ranges.

Most quilt patterns may be made in any color combination that looks good to the seamstress, but there are a few that have traditional colors. The drawings in this book have been shaded to guide the quilter in her choice of colors. Areas shown in black are dark, while the different cross-hatch designs indicate lighter shades and dotted spaces are the lightest of all. Prints are sometimes indicated. A white space indicates that white cloth should be used in that section of the pattern.

The traditions of quilting indicate a Basket Quilt (Fig. 113) is usually brown and white, or yellow and white, for obvious reasons, but there are other traditional combinations not so obvious. A Drunkard's Path (Fig. 206) is usually light blue and white, while W.C.T.U. (Fig. 45) is aways green and white, because those were the colors of the temperance flag. A Jacob's Ladder (Fig. 202) may be made in any shade of blue and white, but it is navy blue and white that is most often used. Patterns of Bear Track (Fig. 83) are usually made in red and white but one may see it in a print on white.

Formerly the making of quilts was very necessary because blankets were not as extensively used then as now. Blankets were expensive as were the huge looms on which they were woven, either of which would entail an exorbitant investment for most families. Also the looms required new wool or cotton yarn, and a separate weaving room added to the house. Quilts used up scraps of cloth that would otherwise be wasted and they could be made by the kitchen fire after the other house-work was finished. But these are not the reasons that quilts were designed with so much color and beauty. For those reasons we must go back to the seamstress. The quilter was, first of all, a woman who cooked, kept house, reared her children, and did all the chores her man had no time to do. We admire the individuality of a Daniel Boone and his kind who could not live in a place where a neighbor was within a day's ride. But what of Mrs. Boone and the other women who always loyally followed their man further and further into the wilderness, away from the small luxuries of the frontier store, a school for the children, or neighbors to talk to? In the summer a woman could have a row of flowers or a flowering bush to attend and feast her eyes upon, but in the winter the world was a cold drab place.

I was speaking on this subject to a lady who was born and reared in Iowa. She said, "Yes, I can look báck fifty years and understand now how it was for Mother. We were just children with a world of corn fields from horizon to horizon in the summer and snow in the winter; seemed all right to us. But Mother was from a small town in Ohio and it must have been hard on her, although she never complained. I can remember her quilts. They were made in reds, blues, yellows, greens, or any variations that were bright and cheerful. She was always working on a new one and I cannot remember a single one that was dark or plain or pastel. She wanted them bright."

They did want them bright. And they did not always use white as a background color. I have a picture of a beautiful Lone Star that has dark green and dark red blocks on a bright yellow background. It stands out, but the colors blend rather than clash.

As late as 1920, quilting was still a popular social function. Not only the large parties such as quilting bees—smaller groups of two or three neighbors meeting over the back fence would talk over new quilt patterns as often as not. It was quite as common for a friend to run over to borrow a certain color quilt scrap, as to borrow the proverbial cup of sugar. No housewife thought her home was complete without a piecebag of quilt scraps hanging from the back of a good comfortable rocker near a good light.

Women were proud to have it said of themselves that they never sat down without something to put their hands to—for "the Devil finds work for idle hands." These women were wiser than we give them credit for, and the harried housewives of today might not be so harried if they took a leaf from their grandmother's book. As any mother knows, when she sits down for a moment with a cup of coffee, that is the exact moment that a favorite toy or book must be found for a child, or a problem needing immediate attention must be attended to for her husband. But a piece of sewing, mending, crocheting, or anything that looks like work will act like magic to give the needed few minutes of rest. No one will want to bother mother when she is so busy. Perhaps such little subterfuges enabled our grandmothers to rear nine children in a huge old house and still smile at the end of the day.

Quilting Bees

One of the most popular social events in a woman's life was the quilting bee. In a day when self-powered machines were unknown or were extremely complicated water-powered gadgets, jobs that were too big for one person or one family were used as an excuse to get the neighbors together for a party. These work parties were commonly called bees. There were house-, barn- and school-raising bees. Road-building bees, corn-husking bees, and many others were quite popular in those days. Quilting, too, fell into this category because of the size of the quilts. A quilt could be quilted by one person over a period of months. A quilt frame requires space at least eight feet square, and there was not enough room in a crowded cabin for such a device. In a larger house there was not a heated room which was not used for family activities. So quilt tops were made in the winter and put away until spring. In warmer weather, the interested persons gathered at a neighbor's home to quilt the tops made during the winter. They set up the frame on a wide porch or the shady lawn of their hostess' home. It is reasonable to assume that rivalries existed as each hostess, in turn, tried to excel the others in the daintiness of her noon repast and the heartiness of her evening meal. The men were invited to the latter meal. Dancing was the usual finish of the quilting bee as well as other types of bees. Many romances must have started at or following quilting parties, since, as the song says "It was from Aunt Dinah's Quilting Party I was seeing Nellie Home."

By the time each woman had had a turn giving a quilting bee, it was fall and time to start sewing tops again.

The children also loved these quilting bees because their mothers took them along and they could play together all day. My father-in-law tells of the quilting bees his mother held in her front yard. The family lived in a farm house with a wide 'L'-shaped porch. Two or three quilting frames were set up on this porch. The children played around and under the porch and tried to listen to the ladies' talk. He said the children never really understood much of the conversations because just as the ladies got to the interesting point they would whisper.

A lady who used to spend her summers with her grandmother in North Carolina said that the ladies there tied their quilts. The children were invaluable at these quilting bees. They were stationed below the quilting frames to return the needles after the ladies stuck them down through the quilt.

The Marriage Quilt

An old English custom was continued in Baltimore and became quite popular. The custom was for a bride-elect to have a "baker's dozen" quilts handmade by herself, as well as the rest of her linens and all of her clothing. These were to last her through the first years of marriage until she had daughters old enough to help make more linens. In order to have all of her quilts ready by her wedding day she usually had her first quilt finished by the time she was seven years old. One of the first refinements of this old custom decreed that a girl who was as yet not "spoken for" (not engaged) could not use love symbols such as cupids, doves, love knots, and hearts on her quilts. The Marriage Quilt, usually the last and most elaborate one, often carried a generous quantity of these symbols, since it was used on the marriage bed for a spread as long as she lived. Thus such a quilt could only be made after a girl was engaged.

In the 1700s a fad for cut paper pictures and novelties swept the colonial cities. Young ladies asked their future husbands to cut out a pattern to be used in making the Marriage Quilt. Soon this became a regular custom without regard for whether the young man had artistic ability. This custom prevailed in Baltimore and other eastern cities until the Civil War took a great many young men away from home for long periods of time. The custom was not revived following the Civil War.

Usually a bride finished all of her linen herself with only the occasional assistance of her mother or other relatives. In the areas previously referred to during the late 1700s, the bride-elect frequently asked her friends to help quilt the wedding quilt just before the wedding. At the same time the linens and bridal finery could be shown. Slowly the occasional party grew into a settled custom. The superstition then grew that just as

354. *This old turkey-red and white top was made around the turn of the century. Nothing is known about it, not even its name, because it was found in an antique shop.*

bad luck happened to the girl who worked on a layette before she had the right to do so, bad luck would happen to the engaged girl who sewed on her own Marriage Quilt. In addition to helping quilt the Marriage Quilt, each friend of the bride-elect would make a quilt patch and sign her name in India ink or embroidery. This frequently included the date and sometimes a verse of poetry. All the friends would then meet at the bride-elect's home, sew the patches together, quilt the top and present the quilt to the prospective bride as a wedding present. This custom spread all over the United States as people moved westward. Around the turn of the century, 1900, the making of a Marriage Quilt became less popular. Instead, friends of the bride substituted small household items rather than quilt patches. The Marriage Quilt is now a thing of the past but friends of the bride still meet to give her presents before the wedding. This, I believe, is the origin of the bridal shower.

Friendship Quilts

Friendship Quilts were very much like wedding quilts. A group of women made patches and later met to sew them together and quilt the top thus made. The finished quilt was presented to a person the group wished to honor. It may have been a retiring minister, teacher, a family leaving the area, or other persons who had won the admiration of the community. These quilts could be very pretty if the ladies had previously agreed on color, style, and size of the blocks. Generally, however, they did not, which resulted in a hodge-podge of colors, patterns, and sizes. The quilts had a much more sentimental than artistic value, as it was the names and thoughts of old friends that made these quilts popular.

One of my friends, now in her seventies, has a Friendship Quilt made for her mother when she was married. The pupils of a private school in which the mother taught some years before gave her the quilt as a wedding present. The quilt was highly prized both by the mother and the daughter. It is now a treasured possession of the third and fourth generation since some of the teenage girls whose signatures are on the quilt became actresses and wives of public figures.

In one part of New England during the latter half of the 19th century, any young man leaving home for the West received a quilt made and signed by his mother and other feminine friends and relatives. These romantic Victorians thought that seeing their names and good wishes in a distant place might keep the young impressionable man safe from evil influences, and who is to say it did not?

Superstitions Surrounding Quilts

One of the oddest superstitions that grew up around quilt-making was brought back from the Orient on the China Clippers. According to the superstition, only God could create a perfect thing and if a human produced an object without some flaw, it would call the Devil and misfortune would follow. For this reason some quilts were made with a blue leaf or green flower in the design, to offset the evil. These quilts usually date from the early eighteen hundreds.

A quilt pattern that had a superstition surrounding it was one called Wandering Foot (Fig. 341). A superstitious woman would never allow this pattern to be used on a quilt to cover a boy's bed. Wandering foot was a colloquial expression for wanderlust. The evil influence of this quilt was supposed to be so great that any male sleeping under it would soon leave home. However, it was fragile as most superstitions are; a woman simply had to name her quilt Turkey Tracks to render the superstition ineffective.

Quilt Symbolism

Symbols were very important to quilters. The same era that knew the language of flowers also devised a language of quilts. Pineapples (Fig. 342) denoted hospitality. They were considered lucky and able to bring friends closer. The Dove (Fig.

343) in the early 1800s, symbolized femininity and a happy marriage. A group of young ladies was called a "dove party" which certainly is a much more dignified term than our contemporary "hen party." For thousands of years the Swastika (Figs. 13, 344) was a symbol of good fortune and fertility to many races of men until it was given the more sinister meaning during the Second World War. Flowers, when used on a quilt, had the same meaning as in a bouquet. Red roses meant love, lilies meant purity and daisies meant innocence.

In the olden days a woman displayed only those quilts of which she could boast that she had put in every stitch herself. These quilts were laid carefully, one on top of the other, on the best company bed, where they were removed and folded, one at a time, and incidentally admired, by the guest before he or she could retire. It was reported that even Martha Washington, a very fine needlewoman, kept between fifteen and twenty quilts displayed in this way.

X

DATING AN OLD QUILT

How is the age of a quilt determined if it is not known when it was made and by whom? This is frequently asked of those who have made a systematic study of the subject. It is also a question that confronts collectors and curators of museums in order that a quilt's history and period may be established. Obviously, this question does not arise if the quilter had worked the date and her identity into the quilt or had otherwise indelibly marked it. Failing this, the following paragraphs offer possible solutions.

The Name of the Quilt

The name given to a quilt, if it is known from family records, can be useful in dating it. A rose pattern named Whig Rose would have to be made before 1835 after which it could be called Democrat or Republican Rose, or if Biblical names were popular Rose of Sharon. Today if I were to make a quilt from an old Rose pattern, I would make it of orange material and call it Jiminy Cricket for my favorite rose bush. This bush is named after the cricket in the children's book *Pinnochio*. In about a hundred years people could be puzzled over the inconsistency of naming a rose pattern after a character in a children's book, for the Jiminy Cricket rose would, in all probability, be forgotten.

My favorite enigmas of this sort are the patterns Brown Goose (Fig. 71) and the Pennsylvania Design (Fig. 355). When explaining the Brown Goose other writers have mentioned the old folk song the first lines of which are, "Go tell Aunt Rhody her old grey goose is dead." It is still difficult to understand why this patch was named after a goose. It would be interesting if someone explained what the flower is intended to represent in the Pennsylvania Design. Usually such flowers were a simplification of those common to the garden or fields and are easily recognized, but this one remains a puzzle.

Dating the Cloth

The second method is by establishing the date of the cloth used in the quilt. All during the Colonial period cloth used in quilts was either homespun or was imported, usually from England or France. These imported cloths are a study in themselves and it would be well to read such books as *America's Fibers* by Bendure and Pfiffer (1946), or *Man Is a Weaver* by Baily (1949). Homespun cloth is easily identified because the human hand cannot apply equal pressures at all times. The handspun thread shows irregularities which recur randomly. When this thread is used in weaving, the irregularities cannot form a pattern. Also on hand looms the weaving is tighter at some places and looser at others. The irregularities cannot be successfully copied by machines because the machines form repeated patterns. Machines are not capable of producing an infinite number of variations. Any quilt with homespun backing or made entirely of homespun, vegetable-dyed fabric would have had to be made before 1820. After that time factory fabricated cloth became available in the United States.

In printed materials a knowledge of history is invaluable because the things people were interested in and enthusiastic over usually found their way into cloth patterns. As an example, a piece of cloth bearing a portrait of Andrew Jackson could not have been used before General Jackson became sufficiently prominent following the Battle of New Orleans in

January, 1815, for the manufacturers to be sure that this cloth would sell. It would take a month or more after the battle was fought for the news to reach Washington, D.C. and be spread to the rest of the country. The cloth makers would then have to make the cloth and distribute it before women could buy it. It would be in the latter part of 1815 or early in 1816 before a quilt could be made of this cloth.

A knowledge of dress fashions is also helpful. For a number of years large floral patterns were popular. During other years, stripes, spots, or checks were the fashion. Most of the pieces in a quilt will be remnants from dressmaking.

I have a sample of an advertisement of a dry goods store dated August 17, 1825. It lists the following goods for sale:

> Angola Cassimeres
> Plain and Striped Satinettes
> Bombazets and Bombazeens
> Irish Popolins
> Striped Bengals
> Blue and Yellow Company Nankeens
> Levantine, Senshaws, Mantuas
> Florence and Sarsnett Silks
> Plain and Figured Mull Mull
> Jaconet, Cambrick and Swiss Muslins
> Robinets and Italian Crapes
> Bengal Chintz and Ginghams
> Long Law and Linen Cambricks
> Washington, Wilmington and Union Stripes
> Painted Muslins and Bed Tickings

Surely some of these many fabrics must have found their way into quilts?

Trips to museums and some study in a library will teach one to identify these and many other materials popular through the years.

Daters of quilts should be very thankful that women usually want the very latest for their homes no matter what it is. This induces them to make their quilts from the most fashionable cloth. But there are a few women who save cloth, find it stored in the attic, or perhaps buy it from others who have saved it. This leads to new quilts from cloth that is out of date. Extreme care must be taken not to judge the date of a quilt before all its characteristics have been scrupulously investigated. The backing must be examined. Quilts have been quilted many years after they were pieced. The sewing must be examined. A different hand from that which stitched the top may have quilted the quilt.

The Quilting

The quilting can be used in either of two ways to date the quilt. First, the patterns will conform to those designs which decorate other articles. Fruit was a popular design on fabrics, wood carving on furniture, and popular prints during the early Victorian Age. Its vogue was from about 1820 to 1860. Quilting motifs featuring fruit were very popular during these years. One quilting pattern, the Princess' Feather, has been popular with quilters from the very beginning. The manner in which it is used is a highly individual matter which has changed repeatedly (Figs. 356-362). These feathers vary from simple patterns to very complex ones. The patterns pictured in Figs. 173 and 175 obviously date from 1860 for they are awkward and rather intricate as were most of the designs of that period. The pattern in Fig. 165 just has to go with the cozy nooks and Turkish Tables of the 1890s.

Second, the stitches themselves are the next clue to the age of a quilt. Tiny, regular stitches that do not vary in length by more than the length of one thread in the fabric clearly state that the quilt was made before 1820 except in very rare cases. In colonial days one of the main parts of a little girl's education was the one or two hours each day she spent learning to sew. She had to make each stitch and each space just so long. To do this she counted the threads in the material as she sewed. Three years of age was considered the correct time to begin learning to sew. By the time the child became a woman, practice had perfected her sewing into almost machine-like regularity but

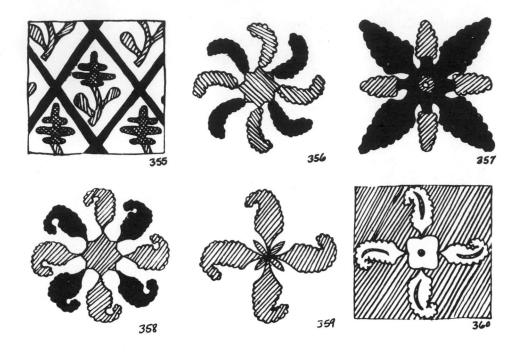

355. *Pennsylvania Design*   356. *Princess' Feather (1835)*   357. *Princess' Feather*   358. *Princess' Feather*   359. *Princess' Feather (1840)*   360. *Princess' Feather*

with a daintiness and freedom that put any machine sewing to shame. Once these stitches have been seen they will never be forgotten, nor mistaken, for other methods of teaching women to sew are not so painstaking. I have seen many quilts where the stitches are still strong and good although the cloth has worn so completely that only a few threads are caught in the stitches to identify the color of the patch.

Location

The section of the country where a quilt was made, if known, will help in dating an appliqué quilt. The appliqué quilt was never very popular in the North. It wasted too much time and took too much material. In the South, however, when wealth and slaves gave women more leisure and where fewer quilts were needed due to the shorter, warmer winters, appliqué quilts were made to set off the great poster beds in lovely southern homes. During the 1870s with their "cult of wealth" preoccupation, the appliqué quilt moved north, to be made up and shown off by the fashionable ladies of that day. The association of the appliqué quilt with wealth may have created the notion that a pieced quilt looks at home on a maple bedroom set, while an appliquéd quilt seems to call for a mahogany suite. There were a few appliquéd quilts made in the North before 1870, especially in Pennsylvania or New York State by ladies who had contacts in the South. But these were only the wealthy ladies who made a few appliquéd quilts, probably just enough to prove their skill. Likewise in the South many pieced quilts were made by people who could ill-afford the waste of the appliqué quilts and the pieced quilts of the mountain women of West Virginia and Tennessee are famous for their beauty.

Size May Help Date a Quilt

Quilts made before the middle of the nineteenth century were often eight to ten feet square. They needed to be that large to cover beds made to sleep three people, and to conceal a trundle bed slid under them in the daytime. Feather

361. *Princess' Feather*

362. *Princess' Feather*

363. *Circular Saw* (1842)

364-366. Patterns dating to 1842, names unknown.

beds or husk mattresses that were several inches thick were used on these beds which increased their height. These beds required a small stepstool of two or three stairs to allow one to climb into them. Quilts used on these beds needed to be correspondingly large; however, the new king-size beds of today need quilts almost as large as those nineteenth century quilts.

The Filler

The filler may also be used to date a quilt. Because of the shortages in the early colonies, quilts were often filled with leaves, grass, feathers, bark, and other odd materials. However, with time and rough usage these quilts are probably extinct and it is doubtful if one would be called upon to date such a quilt. A few quilts in early Colonial days were filled with wool although this was not a popular custom. Wool was much too valuable when made into cloth to permit using the fleece for quilt filler. Cotton was the usual filler.

Cotton in a quilt can indicate three things. If there are seeds left in the cotton filler the quilt was stuffed with hand-carded cotton. The seeds may be seen by holding the quilt up before a light. The tiny black specks in the cotton are the seeds. Seeds in a quilt indicate that the quilt must have been made before the era when the cotton gin was in general use for separating the seeds from the cotton. Eli Whitney perfected his gin in

1793 and ginned cotton became plentiful in the next 10 to 20 years. Hand carding cotton is a tedious job, and was performed in as short a time as possible. When the number of seeds in the cotton filler are few and there are large areas quite free of seeds, the quilt is a southern quilt. Many seeds in the cotton means that it is a northern quilt. The northern housewife did most of her own work with the help of her daughters or in some cases with the aid of only one or two servants. It was not possible for her to devote much of her time, or that of others, to painstakingly remove all the seeds from a few pounds of cotton. However, in the South there was usually a slave or two that might be kept busy in odd moments de-seeding cotton. In this manner the southern housewife could afford to be fussy about her cotton filler.

Dating the Blocks and Borders

The patterns of the blocks, border, and the way they are set together went through phases also. I have dated as many of the patterns and borders shown in this book as possible with the earliest dates available. See Chapter III on the history of quilt patterns in America.

367-368. *Patterns dating to 1842, names unknown*   369. *Whig Rose (1814)*

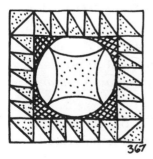

367   368   369

Checking the Colors

The colors and phases of popularity are recorded in Chapter IX. The simplest ones to date are the quilts with pieces of dark-flowered prints that were popular during the Civil War. The red, green, and white quilts were popular during the 1840s. The red and white quilts reached their peak of popularity in the 1890s through the early 1900s. Care must be taken with these last two color combinations since they have been popular since the years they were first made. The quilting pattern and other features should be carefully examined to determine if they agree with an early date before assigning it to one of these quilts. A good way to tell a very early red and green on white when the other signs are favorable, is that the earlier the pattern the more green and the less red there will be on the quilt. The red and white quilts were made by our grandmothers and great-grandmothers. Most of these are still in the families of the women who made them which makes it easier to date than most quilts. Care must be taken when buying one to see that it was not made recently since they are still very popular among older quilters.

Patterns for Quilt Blocks

What has been said about cloth patterns and quilting patterns is also true about the patterns used for the quilt blocks. Figs. 363 through 368 are from a dated quilt block collection given to a bride in 1842 by her friends and relatives. The collection has remained in the same family to this day. Several of the patterns can be easily traced to the 1840s but the most revealing is Fig. 363 which looks like nothing but a circular saw blade. Joseph T. Butler in a book called *American Antiques 1800-1900* tells us:

"While the circular saw was known during the eighteenth century, it was not until the 1840s that it came into increased use."

If the collection were not already dated this would be an invaluable clue. However, it was useful in confirming the family story that the entire collection was assembled at one time.

If each of the above categories are taken into consideration, or as many of them as are available, and compared with the earliest and latest dates each could have been used, the probable date of the quilt may be found by elimination within ten years or less.

As an illustration of how this works, I give the procedure I used a few years ago to date a quilt. It was the Whig Rose (Fig. 369).

The quilt was a lovely appliquéd rose pattern in red and green on white. The material was homespun including the embroidery thread used for stems. The vegetable-dyed colors had faded to a soft rose and green without becoming very light in tone. The quilt when held up to the light showed seeds in the cotton. The quilting was very fine.

The quilt was owned by an elderly woman who was the last of a family that had owned and lived on a Pennsylvania farm before the Revolutionary War. She knew that the quilt had been made by one of her ancestors and that it was not a Rose of Sharon.

It was not only necessary to determine the date of this quilt, but since it was to be displayed, it was also necessary to determine its name. This was my reasoning:

1. The homespun hand-dyed cotton cloth indicates the quilt must have been made prior to 1820.

2. There were too many seeds in the filler for this to be a southern quilt.

3. The pattern was appliquéd even though by all signs the quilt was northern; therefore, the family was affluent at the time this quilt was made.

4. The family must have been able to observe southern culture because the appliqués were distinctly southern for many years after the colonial period. Thus this quilt had to be made after travel became easier in the colonies after the Revolutionary War. This establishes the tentative date between 1790 and 1820.

5. During the thirty years 1790 to 1820, the most important subject in public minds was politics. This knowledge plus the fact that it must have been an affluent farm family, led to the reasoning that this was probably a Whig Rose pattern.

6. All of the above reasoning plus the fine sewing, the colors and the general appearance of the quilt resulted in establishing a tentative date of between 1812 and 1816.

About a year after I was called in to date her quilt the lady found an old diary when she went through some trunks in the attic. It was the diary of the woman who had made the quilt and she had listed and described all of the fancy work she had done. I was gratified to learn that the diary confirmed the name as Whig Rose and gave 1814 as the year it was made.

Fashions Are a Clue

A knowledge of the popular opinions and fashions of the day as reflected in contemporaneous publications is invaluable. For example:

Mrs. Pullman, New York needlework authority in the magazine, *The Ladies' Manual of Fancy Work,* 1858, recommending the use of silk, velvet or satin for quilts, writes:

> "Of the patchwork with calico, I have nothing to say. Valueless indeed must be the time of that person who can find no better use for it than to make counterpanes and quilts of pieces of cotton. Emphatically is the proverb true of cotton patchwork, 'Le jeu ne vaut pas la chandelle.' It is not worth either the candle or the gaslight."

In a magazine article on needlework in 1960 came this statement:

> "In the last 50 years quilt-making in general has degenerated to the extent, that most women who plan a top, sew an appliqué patch on a square of white, embroider around the appliqué and join these together either with or without strips of different color. These quilts come out looking like assembly-line products like our cars or mass-produced table-

cloths because almost all the women use one of four designs —'Butterflys', 'Sunbonnet Sue', 'Overhaul Sam', or 'Sailboats'."

As may be seen it would take a very strong-minded woman indeed to make cotton patchwork in 1858, or one of the appliqué patterns in 1960 because these experts were only echoing the prevailing opinions of their day and there is nothing as dead as yesterday's fashions. A knowledge of fashions is indispensable when a quilt is to be dated, especially when there is a long period of time between the possible dates during which the quilt could have been made. The prevailing mood—quiet, exuberant, or sad—are echoed in the quilts of each period.

Today's quilts will be easy to date in the future because of the present preoccupation with antiques and American history. Women are copying all of the older quilt patterns, and the older the pattern the more popular it is. However, the sewing is modern; in some cases women are using their sewing machines to copy the old quilts. Also the older quilts were made either wholly or in part of homespun materials. The new quilts with their modern fabrics cannot be confused with the older ones.

370A. *Antique quilt patches used as wall decorations in a bedroom.*

370B. *Antique quilt used as a wall hanging in a modern living room.*

XI

DESIGNER'S BOUTIQUE

As long as quilts have been made, the techniques of appliquéing, piecing, and quilting have been used for many other purposes, such as clothing and items to beautify every room in the home.

One of the most famous of these other purposes was the making of petticoats for the lovely dresses with divided skirts worn by ladies during the 1550 to 1800 era. Samuel Pepys, the diarist, tells of a maid servant who stole his best quilt, ran away, and when found had made it into a fashionable petticoat. Fancy vests worn by gentlemen during the 1550 to 1800 era were also often quilted.

Sewing pockets were used by the ladies who wore divided skirts. The pockets, or a pair of them, were tied around the waist and covered each hip. When donning overdress, the side panels hid the pockets. This was a very useful item of apparel when dresses were not equipped with pockets.

Trapunto or Italian Quilting

For those not familiar with trapunto, this is a little-known

159

type of quilting and is used primarily for collars, cuffs, pockets, and other trimming.

Trapunto quilting is a simple form of quilting that eliminates the usual cotton filler. The material chosen may be of any firm, tightly-woven fabric; cotton, linen, silk, satin, or any of the similarly woven synthetic cloths. Within this group of materials, velvet may also be included. A plain-colored fabric or one with a single printed motif large enough to fill the entire face of the object to be made, is best. Materials with small scattered patterns detract from the larger trapunto design. Trapunto designs must be large, simple ones; flowers, baskets of flowers, and scrolls are the most desirable. The large printed motif should be stitched on its own outline and then padded from underneath. The backing may be of any light, loosely-woven fabric. If the article is to receive much wear, unbleached muslin may be used. For small, lightweight articles such as collars and cuffs or trimming for wearing apparel, cheesecloth may be used as this eliminates bulkiness.

Diag. 21   *Diag. 22*

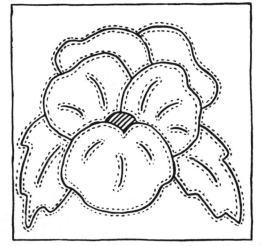
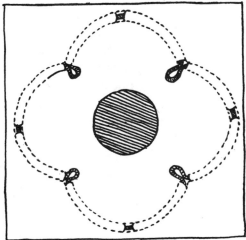

The backing material is basted to the back of the face. A simple outline design is then drawn on the backing. In some cases a picture may be copied by first placing the picture and backing over a strong light source, such as a window, to trace the picture. Diagram 21 shows the design drawn with solid lines. The broken lines on each side of the solid lines represent sewn lines in running stitch ⅛ inch from the drawn lines for a total of ¼ inch apart. The shaded portion of the design should be padded.

A large, blunt yarn needle is used to push the yarn between the two sewn lines. *Orlon bulky yarn rather than wool yarn is recommended as Orlon does not shrink* when washed in hot water. If wool yarn is used, care should be taken in laundering to avoid shrinkage. The following steps are recommended to obtain the best results with this type of work:

1. With the yarn threaded through the blunt yarn needle and starting at one corner, draw the yarn between the top and backing and the two lines of stitches.

2. Do not knot the end of the yarn. Leave two or three inches of free yarn.

3. Run the needle through the trough until the needle extends through the backing.

4. Draw up the slack yarn and make another stitch into the hole made by the needle where it came through the backing as near the previous hole as possible. The small space thus created will not show on the right side of the material.

5. At a sharp corner in the design, as at Diagram 22, leave a small loop of yarn. Should the yarn shrink for some reason, the loop will ease itself into the trough thus preventing puckering of the design.

Modern Uses

Quilting, appliquéing and piecing can be used in many ways to brighten a modern home or wardrobe. Quilted materials seem right in Early American rooms furnished with maple furniture (Fig. 371). Danish and other modern furniture de-

371. *A quilt was used to upholster the settee, chair and valance in this drawing. The quilted pieces might have been made especially for the furniture, thus eliminating the broken designs.*

pend on the texture of rugs, curtains, and other fabric around them to give them warmth and livability and the textures of quilted, appliquéd, and pieced fabrics are ideal for decorating this type of modern room.

These techniques can be used in making many articles for the living room, from pillow tops to furniture upholstery. Crazy-quilt throws, small appliquéd pictures, curtains, draperies, chair sets or antimacassars, bookcovers, hassocks, and cardtable covers are other ideas.

Basic Directions for Making Small Articles

Follow the directions given in Chapters V and VI for making quilts. However, a much smaller quilting frame will be required for the smaller items. Only long curtains or draperies would require the large quilting frames. Quilt hoops, hooked rug frames or merely a frame made of two pairs of 1 x 2-inch boards, one pair four feet long, the other pair five feet long, may be used. These may be fastened at the corners with "C" clamps. All three frames are readily stored when not in use or can usually be set against a wall or in a closet without removing the material being quilted.

Diag. 23

Unbleached muslin has been used for the backing in every article shown in this chapter. As explained earlier, when two fabrics are combined, the weaker fabric will wear first and seems to take wear from the stronger fabric, making it last longer. Thus the fabric used as a backing should be weaker or at least no stronger than the facing material. When badly worn, the backing may be replaced.

Pillows

Any square quilt pattern (I like them 12 inches or more) can be made into a pillow. There are also pretty patterns in round, oval or hexagon shapes. You may use the patterns on both sides of the pillow or use plain fabric for the back. If the pillow is large enough, the two sides can be placed together with a fringe or corded trim between them. You may also place a two- or three-inch wide band of plain or pieced material as the boxed sides of the pillow between the top and bottom.

Wall Hangings

We are using more imagination in decorating the walls of our homes. The popular wall hangings are easily made from cloth. I have made up two striking wall hangings by combining a dark and a light pieced design for background to contrast with a colorful appliqué.

The first is made by piecing eight Orange Peel squares, 12 inches by 12 inches, in black and white. Over this is appliquéd a Love Apple design 3 feet by 1½ feet wide in red, yellow, and green.

The second wall hanging is made of eight 12-inch square Shoo-fly designs in navy blue and white with a large Daffodil

Vase in light blue, yellow, and green, appliquéd to it.

To make the large patterns see the directions on page 78; for pieced patterns see pages 84-85 for the appliqué designs. Line the finished hangings with muslin and make hems in the top and bottom to hold two dowels, one ⅜ inch, the other ¼ inch, with the larger one at the top. The ends of the dowels may be decorated or you may use fancy curtain rods. A gold cord can be tied to each end of the top dowel to allow you to hang this decoration on the wall.

Tote Bags

One of the newest fashions is the tote bag which is carried on one arm or over the shoulder as a shopping or needlework bag. The outside may be of any material in any color, the inside should be of heavy, long-wearing fabric like unbleached muslin or even denim. You will be more satisfied with these bags if you use plain rather than print fabrics, as the design will show up much better on the plain material.

Wearing Apparel

Since the introduction of central heating, quilted clothing has not been required for warmth in the home. However, quilted garments made of very thin fabrics with a very light layer of cotton padding are popular in winter. A few of the garments that might be made for women or girls are skirts, jackets, hats, robes, purses, fitted capes, skating skirts, and hooded jackets. Baby sets of bonnet, jacket and bootees might match a quilted blanket. Men and boys could use quilted vests, bulky lounging robes and sport jackets.

372. *The patterns for the five small pillows are: Young Man's Fancy, House on the Hill, The Basket, Streak O'Lightening, and The Sailboat.*

373. *And the three large pillows: The Windmill, Full-Blown Rose, and Double Pinwheel.*

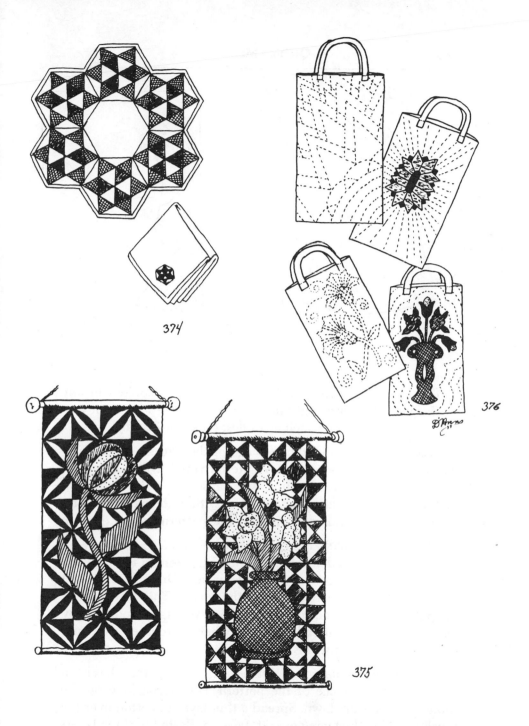

374. *The design on the place mat and napkin is Star Design.* 375. *The two wall hangings combine pieced and appliqué designs in a colorful medley.* 376. *Fancy tote bags can be made from many appliqué, pieced, or quilted designs.*

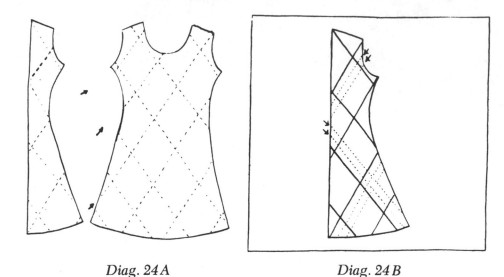

Diag. 24 A   *Diag. 24 B*

The general directions given below may be applied to any of the garments with slight modification. Select a garment pattern without trimming such as ruffles, tucks, or inserts.

CUTTING DIRECTIONS: Cut each piece of the pattern twice, once for the facing and once of the material which will be used for the backing. Because quilting will cause a certain amount of shrinkage, cut the pattern slightly larger than the paper pattern.

Stay-stitch around each piece of the pattern as it is cut out.

MARKING THE QUILTING PATTERN: When each piece has been cut out and stay-stitched, mark the quilting pattern on the backing.

Lay the pieces together on a flat surface, Diagram 24A, and match the quilting pattern across the seams. This matching of the pattern at the seams illustrates the advantage of quilting by machine. Material already quilted when purchased does not always match at the seams.

PREPARATIONS FOR QUILTING: When the quilting pattern has been marked on each piece of the pattern, lay the backing on the table, marked side down. Spread a thin layer of cotton over the muslin and lay the facing over it, face up. Baste the three layers together loosely. Appliqué or piece each piece of the pattern separately.

Before beginning to machine quilt, it might be well to reread the chapter on machine sewing quilts.

QUILTING: On the long narrow pieces of a dress pattern, a line of stitching from corner to corner cannot be made. To anchor the three layers, sew a lattice pattern, Diagram 24A. For an intricate pattern stitch on the pattern as near to the lattice pattern as possible. When the lattice is finished, sew two rows of stitches in each direction as is shown by the arrows and dotted lines in Diagram 24B. Continue sewing two lines in each direction until the piece is finished.

FINISHING THE GARMENT: When all of the pieces have been quilted, pull the cotton filler from the seam allowance of each piece and from the hem.

Finish the garment in accordance with the directions given in the pattern.

The beautiful or unusual objects that may be made by piecing, appliquéing, or quilting are limited only by one's own imagination. With imagination and practice comes the ability to turn visions of beauty into reality.

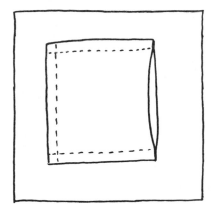

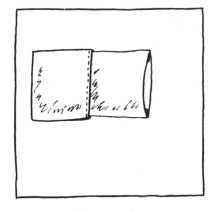

Diag. 25A   Diag. 25B

377. Here is a modern formal dress with trapunto quilting used as the trim. 378. This robe or dressing gown is quilted with a front panel in trapunto quilting for trim. It has matching slippers. 379. Quilted outdoor garments in styles such as this maxi coat and cape are easily made with the instructions on quilting clothing in this chapter. 380. Make a quilted party dress for your teenage daughter for winter.

381. *Jackets and blouses are colorful additions to your wardrobe when pieced like crazy quilts.* 382. *A pieced and quilted Hostess Skirt in the latest style.* 383. *For easy wearing try one of these easy-to-make Ponchos.* 384. *Cape made from a Quilt-As-You-Go pattern in satins and velvet.*

Quilt-As-You-Go Quilts

Ingenuity has been used to great advantage in recent years to invent three new quilting techniques. These, as a class, are called "Quilt-as-you-go quilts" and are made quite differently from other types of quilts. They are put together block by block as they are made and when the top is finished; the quilt, stuffing quilting and all, is finished.

Puffed Quilt

A pattern for the Puffed quilt is just a 4½-inch square. To make a soft, warm quilt cut two 4½-inch squares from cotton cloth. Place these squares face to face and sew around three sides. Turn the block and fold the seam allowance of the open side to the inside. Stuff the pocket thus formed with one clean, used nylon stocking or the equivalent. Make a second pocket just like the first and after turning it, place the closed side of the second pocket inside the open edge of the first about ¼ inch and sew across the two. Stuff the second pocket and repeat.

Cathedral Window Quilt

Use these directions with the diagrams on No. 26. Step 1. (B) Fold all four sides of the seam allowance in ¼ inch (dotted lines). Fold all four corners to the center with the seam allowance inside; overcast the seams. Step 2. Turn the block over. Fold the four corners to the center and tack the points. Make three more of these (C). Step 3. The four plain squares should look like (D). Overcast the edges of the four blocks to make one. Step 4. (E) Place one of the small squares over the above seam in one side. Fold the open edges over the edges of this square and overcast them to hold the small square in place. Repeat this over all the seams in the quilt as you come to them.

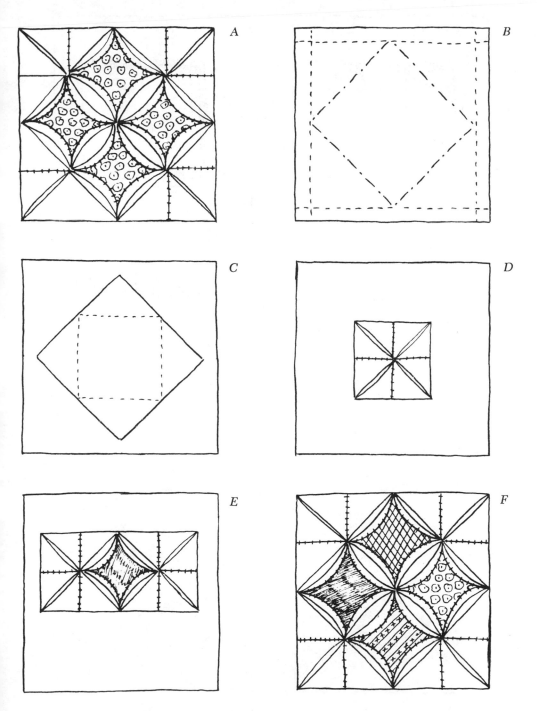

Diag. 26. *Cathedral Window Quilt. The first square* (A) *shows a variation called "Four Leaf Clover". The blocks are made from four 4½-inch plain squares and four 1-inch print squares. The last square* (F) *is the finished Cathedral Window design.*

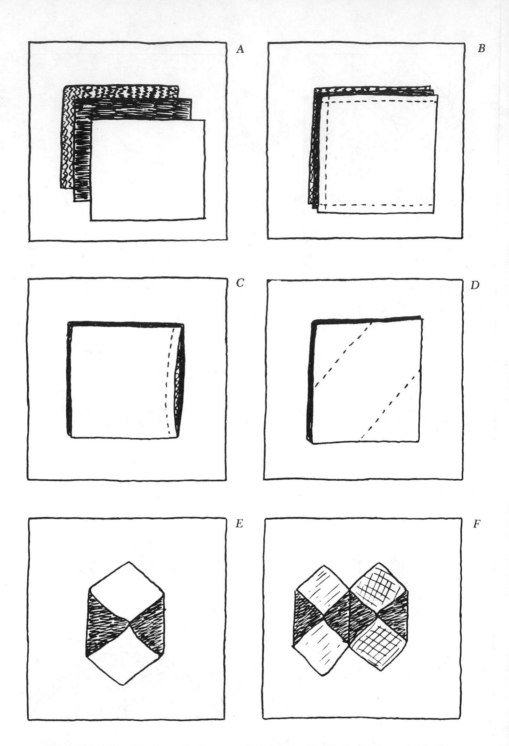

Diag. 27. *This Shadow Quilt is made from eight-inch blocks of black velvet, knit material filling, and bright-colored satins. The cape pictured in Fig. 384 is made from this pattern and lined with black velvet. A quilt would not need the lining. Step 1 (A). Step 2 (B). Step 3 (C). Step 4 (D). The finished block (E). Putting the blocks together (F).*

XII

QUILTING YESTERDAY, TODAY,
AND TOMORROW

There is little doubt about the position quilts held in the past American scene. For warmth, for beauty, and as a good excuse for a social event, most women looked to their quilts. Homes were cold and many quilts were needed. This need lasted in some localities through the World War I era. An article in the *National Geographic Magazine* quoted from an interview with a quilter, who said of her childhood:

> "Only heat was from the fireplace. So cold in the bedrooms we'uns ran real fast to bed and piled on kivers."

Why People Quilt

Of the three principal reasons women had for making quilts in the past, one is no longer valid. Today's homes are too well heated to necessitate many bedcovers. But other reasons for quilting still exist.

A machine can turn out beautiful blankets to be marketed at $3 to $30 apiece. Another machine can sew a quilt in minutes using two pieces of printed cloth and a batt of cotton. Should one of the pieces of cloth happen to have a quilt pattern printed on it—there, a modern-day patchwork quilt is created. It is doubtful, however, that this could be accepted as a real patchwork quilt.

Woman's Day Magazine, July 1962, printed an article on the Pennsylvania Dutch Folk Fair at Kutztown, Pennsylvania which says in part:

"You can also pick up new twists from the ladies who quilt, and those who embroider aprons; from the men and women who paint everyday things such as knife boxes and bread boards with charming old time Pennsylvania Dutch patterns, and from the weavers who follow their own designs on their hand looms. All these are women like yourself whose acquired skills give them great satisfaction. Some ply their crafts for money, but most for the joy of it."

"For the joy of it" is probably the motivating principle behind the "do-it-yourself" trend. The American genius for creating machines has often deprived us of many activities which are the source of much pleasure and satisfaction, for machines have been permitted to take over some of the creative crafts in addition to those involving drudgery.

Many women quilt to make lovely additions to their home furnishings. Certainly, the easiest way to decorate a bedroom would be to make a quilt to match the color scheme. Or, conversely, to match a color scheme to a quilt. As the bed is the focal point of a bedroom, so a quilt becomes the natural focal point for the bedroom decorations.

Sociability is another reason why women made quilts. An interest or hobby is a well-known way for bringing people together. We attend Women's Clubs, P.T.A.'s, and similar meetings and if we are not actively participating in the programs, most of us sit with our hands in our laps listening to the discussion of others. We go home feeling we have accomplished very little. Susan B. Anthony gave some of her first lectures on woman suffrage to women busily engaged in sewing at quilting bees. These women took their ideas home along with their sewing and we enjoy today the political suffrage they achieved while holding their needles in their hands.

In the early days a farm family could be totally self-sufficient when necessary. Even city dwellers raised most of their own food, including meat. In that era girls were taught to sew as a matter of course as soon as their baby fingers could hold a needle. From Pilgrim days to within living knowledge, women were expected to sew all of their clothing. They also made or closely supervised the making of all the linens and bedding needed for their families. Rich or poor, a girl who could not sew a fine seam by the time she was ten was considered a dull or indolent child.

Harriet Beecher Stowe, the author of *Uncle Tom's Cabin,* wrote to her absent husband in 1844, "If I should sew every day for a month to come I should not be able to accomplish a half of what is to be done." Mrs. Stowe was echoing Abigail Adams who wrote a letter to her husband during the Revolutionary War. The letter stated that she "has as much as she can do to provide clothing for the family which would else be naked."

Little girls were started out on straight seams for plain linens like sheets. They were then taught to hem handkerchiefs and embroider small designs. Each stitch they took had to be a certain size; therefore they counted each thread as they sewed. They had an assigned length of time for each day's sewing practice. When each stitch was correct and tiny they were allowed to pick out their first quilt pattern and the pieces to go into it. One glance is sufficient to identify a quilt made before 1850 (Fig. 382), because the stitches are so accurate and tiny, almost as though machine-made.

Martha Washington

Martha Danridge Custis Washington, to give her full name, was taught to sew by her mother when she was a child. She learned to count her stitches. By all accounts, she did not object to sewing with her mother as much as she disliked the arithmetic and spelling lessons from her father. She became a real artist with her needle, although her spelling was always a little uncertain.

On Martha's eleventh birthday her mother gave her a "Housewife" and she later said in a letter that it was one of her favorite gifts. A housewife was a leather roll fitted with scissors, thimble, spools for thread, needles, pin cushion, and other aids to the seamstress.

One year after Valley Forge, on her trip back to Mt. Vernon, Martha Washington stopped at Hunterton, New Jersey. Later, in a letter telling of the visit, her hostess, Mrs. Martha Stewart Wilson, wrote:

"Mrs. Washington told how it had become necessary to make their own domestic cloth, a task at which sixteen spinning wheels were kept constantly busy. She showed me two dresses of cotton striped with silk, 'manufactured by her own domestics'. The silk stripes were made from the ravelings of brown silk stockings and crimson damask chair covers. Her coachman, footman, and waiting maid were all habited in domestic cloth, 'except the coachman's scarlet cuffs and collars'. Those were of imported stuffs."

When George became first president of the new nation, Martha had little time for sewing, because the wives of government officials had to be entertained. The wife of the President found considerably more "state" involved in entertaining than had the wife of the general. Finally, when they could retire to Mt. Vernon to enjoy peacefulness and tranquility, Martha resumed her needlework at her beloved home. A Mrs. Edward Carrington who spent some time at Mt. Vernon in the year 1799 wrote a letter in November to her sister:

"My mornings are spent charmingly . . . then we repair to the old lady's room, which is precisely on the style of our good old Aunt's—that is to say nicely fixed up for all sorts of work . . . on one side sits the chambermaid with her knitting, on the other a little colored pet learning to sew, an old decent woman with her table and shears cutting out the negroes winter clothes, while the good old lady directs them all, incessantly knitting herself, and pointing out to me several pairs of nice colored stockings and gloves she had just finished, and presenting me with a pair half done, she begs me to finish and wear for her sake."

There is no word of Mrs. Washington's quilts, but some of her quilts have been returned to Mt. Vernon for display. One of these quilts is now displayed in the museum. It is a medallion quilt called Penn's Treaty with the Indians.

The center medallion is a copper plate reproduction on linen of the old Penn's Treaty engraving. Around the medallion are concentric rings of chintzes and plain cloth. The second ring is most interesting because it is a fine piece of reverse appliqué. The undercloth is brown and the lattice over it was originally white. Her last quilt top is shown in Fig. 381.

There are fine quilts on the beds in the house; appliquéd, candlewick, and quilted ones, with hangings and matching window curtains, and sometimes matching upholstered chairs.

The spinning room in a separate outside building is most interesting. There are small spinning wheels for linen and wool, and large ones used for cotton thread. There is also a flax break. It was used to beat the flax strands from the rest of the plant. There are wool and cotton cards and many other cloth-making tools on the tables and on the walls.

Among her personal possessions are Mrs. Washington's work basket and quilting frame. The work basket is a dark brown, hand woven, split-cane basket with a high handle and rounded lid. The quilt frame consists of four walnut bars; the larger bars being 11 feet long and one and one-half inches wide with canvas strips for attaching a quilt; the shorter two bars are nine and one-half feet long and two and one-half inches wide. The "C" clamps used today were not available to the colonials. They worked out an arrangement of canvas strips that slid along the bars and could be tightened or loosened by two laces. This frame is too big to be on display at present.

All of the quilts shown at Mt. Vernon are from the colonial period and are of the European type. The wealthy and socially prominent people used these European types of quilts until after the Revolutionary War when everything English was in great disfavor. It was then that they switched to making the American type of quilt that the poor and middle class ladies had been evolving for about one hundred years.

Mary Pickersgill

During the Revolutionary War when General Washington was in Philadelphia, he commissioned a battle flag for himself.

It was based on the English flag and was called "The Grand Union Flag." The General carried this flag all during the first years of the war. A quilter named Rebecca Young who made this flag was one of those women like Betsy Ross who made "colours" for ships and army regiments. In 1807 Rebecca and her daughter, Mary Pickersgill, a widow who was also a "colours maker," moved with Mary's small daughter Caroline to the maritime city of Baltimore. They bought a house fronting on the harbour at the corner of Pratt and Albemarle Streets.

This provided a location for successfully merchandising Mary's colours with the ship captains.

Shortly after Mary Pickersgill was given publicity in the Baltimore Directory as a maker of "ship's banners and flags," Colonel George Armistead, then in command of Ft. McHenry, needed a new flag "big enough so the British would be sure to see it" during the War of 1812. Mary's brother-in-law, Commodore Joshua Barney, and General John Sticker asked her to make it.

Mary made the flag in time for the British attack on Ft. McHenry in September 1814 even though it took nearly a year to complete. Aged Rebecca, thirteen year old Caroline, and two nieces also assisted in weaving the 400 yards of cloth or bunting. They dyed the cloth and cut it into fifteen red and white stripes. They cut fifteen white stars and a field of blue. They sewed these pieces together by hand into a flag 30 feet by 42 feet weighing 180 pounds when finished.

The house has been restored as the "Star Spangled Banner House," which cannot be described better than in the information sheet which says:

"This house is not furnished as a museum, but as it might have been when it was the home of this family of women with their strong patriotic heritage. This is a tiny house, one of the few, if not the only, city row house of the period on exhibition."

The furniture in this house is of the Sheraton and Adams period and is carefully matched in good taste with the few Pickersgill pieces in the collection. The house passed from Mary to her daughter Caroline who died without heirs in 1857. The furnish-

382. *This red print on white homespun was made around 1820. The quilting is especially fine. (Star Spangled Banner House, Baltimore, Maryland.)*

ings were then dispersed at her death and the quilts now in the house are of the period when Mary and Caroline were alive, but were made by other Baltimore ladies. However, all three of the Pickersgill women were fine seamstresses and in the custom of that day they must have made all their own quilts. The quilts on display are well worth studying because they are in the proper setting which helps to bring the Federal period to life (see Figs. 6 and 382).

Family Quilts

At the time this chapter was begun, I had a definite outline in mind. It was my plan to give names of famous women who quilted from the pre-Revolution period to the present. The first, of course, was Martha Washington. It soon became evident that it would be difficult to make further selections on the premise of fame alone since fame may be placed in any one of several categories. As an example, although Mrs. Pickersgill's flag was famous, her name was familiar to only a few people. There were those who were prominent in contemporary social activities and social reforms. It must not be overlooked that there were many who were famous only to their families. In the light of the above desire to single out famous quilters, I resolved to select a few because of their particular prominence.

Mrs. Jefferson Davis quilted for her family during the Civil War. A letter written by one of her friends to another in September 1866 states:

"Varine (Mrs. Davis) wanted a piece of colored silk from one of Mrs. Johnson's dresses (wife of Confederate General Joseph Johnson) for a quilt she was making that was to tell the story of the Confederacy—Mrs. Clay called it her 'immortal patchwork.' Each square was to be a memory of better days."

In Salt Lake City the early Mormon women were busy. From a book on the early days in Nevada, a passage about Brigham Young's family house states:

"Quilting frames and spinning wheels were in steady use producing quilts and yarn for children's attire."

From a recent quilting pattern book printed in California comes this story of a pioneer woman and her quilt:

"This quilt . . . was made in 1829. It was in a bride's chest that was carried by an ox team from Kentucky to California during the gold rush in 1853. The poles fastened to the wheels of the wagon to float it across the streams must not have been successful for the chest with its precious contents was thrown into a stream and water soaked. The stains are on the quilt yet."

On a trip through New York State I found two old quilts on a shelf in a home where I spent the night. When the owner was asked about them, she said that they had been made by her husband's grandmother when she was a young woman. The owner did not think they were at all valuable but said she kept them because they had great sentimental value to her family. This is a typical case of many quilts that were made in the last one hundred years. They are valued much more for their connection with the past than they are as utilitarian objects. Almost every household in the United States has an old "quilt that grandma made." These are brought out in succeeding generations and shown to each child. In this manner the quilt and its story is passed along from generation to generation.

In my family, the most treasured quilt was lost two generations ago. I have heard the story so often from my mother that I can hardly realize that I have never seen it. In my mother's words:

"My great-grandmother, your great-great-grandmother, was an artist with her needle. She could take a picture of an animal or bouquet of flowers and copy it perfectly in embroidery, just by looking at it. She made a quilt for my mother from pieces of stiff silk and velvet (a crazy quilt). On the large pieces she embroidered a bouquet of flowers, on pieces a little smaller she embroidered animals, birds, and butterflies, and on the very smallest pieces she embroidered a single flower.

Each piece was outlined with a decorative embroidery stitch. But the most wonderful thing of all to us children was that the eye of each animal and bird and the center of each flower was a black bead. Mother kept this quilt put away in her cedar chest. The only time it was ever brought out was when one of the children was ill; then we would look at it for hours and tell each other stories about the different patches. When I was nine we lived in Tustin, Michigan where Papa owned the Hotel. They had a lot of trouble with the railroads back then because the locomotives were woodburning and if they were not careful they could lose the spark screen from the stack of the engine and sparks would spray everything along the right-of-way. The railroads went through the middle of Tustin at that time and cut Main Street in two. The fire department was on the other side of the tracks and when a train stopped at the station or warehouses it completely blocked the road between the two halves of town. One day in August a train without its chimney screen stopped to unload freight, a shower of sparks fell and before the trainmen would move the train, half of Tustin was destroyed. The chief method they had in those days of fighting fires was to douse blankets and quilts in water and throw them on a roof. Our beloved quilt was thrown on a roof and burned before mother's eyes. My great-grandmother had died shortly before this time and I don't think my mother ever really got over the loss of her quilt. Anyway we left Tustin and Michigan shortly afterward."

I have in my collection another quilt top that was made by this same great-great-grandmother shortly before she died at ninety years of age. (Fig. 227.)

The Enjoyment of Quilt-Making

In the book *Dolls of Three Centuries* the author, Eleanor St. George, digresses to tell a story of her childhood.

"When the author of this book and her sister, Frank, two years younger, were small girls, it was a joy to them to nestle down in their mother's bed before going to their own bed at night and listen to stories suggested to her by the old prints in the pieced quilt on her bed. Whose dress had that print been? When was it bought? Where? Who made it? How was it made, and where was it first worn?"

It is no wonder the family quilts are esteemed so highly by us since they form a major part of our childhood memory. I have seen dignified, elderly men look at a quilt with a suspicion of tears in their eyes because the pattern resembled a quilt their mothers had worked on when they were boys.

Are quilts really difficult to make? This book has endeavored to show that more time is required than work. Up to the first quarter of this century little girls were usually taught to quilt as a matter of course. To test the children of today, I invited three neighborhood girls to learn quilt-making during a summer vacation. The youngest was seven, the oldest nine. All the girls finished their quilts and tied them.

Rose Wilder Lane in a recent series of articles in *Woman's Day Magazine* on American Needlework, expressed it perfectly:

"If you use a traditional pattern you needn't even think about it after you've cut out the pieces. You cut out dozens of them, using sharp shears and a stiff pasteboard pattern piece; you stack the colors neatly in piles. Then you thread the needle and settle comfortably in your chair. The needle runs easily back and forth through soft cloth while nerves relax and useless worries fade away. Smoothing out a finished block, you have a pleasant sense of achievement. You are making a thing of beauty that generations to come will prize.

"Or, brisk and busy you may hum while you feed long strips of patches through the humming machine. Snip them apart, set them together and run them through again; you may make a whole quilt top between lunch time and bringing the children home from school. This will horrify some, but I was a pioneer child; I know how the Pilgrim women would have welcomed the machine, incredulously, admired its swiftness and its perfect stitches and thanked God for easing women's work. Whether your tool is a needle or tamed electricity, your patchwork is your own; you express yourself in patterns and colors and way of working."

As for the women who work, if there are children in the family, extra leisure time should be spent with them. Sitting in a comfortable chair sewing for an hour while the children tell of their exciting day or show off their reading skills would not be time wasted.

Quilting as Therapy

There are people who need an occupation. These include the elderly, many of the handicapped, and the ill. My attention was attracted to a picture in a newspaper of a white-haired lady holding a quilt. The headline read, "Busy Grandmother Follows Old Craft." Here, in part, is what the article said:

"Mrs. Mary ...., 84, is blind. Mrs. .... keeps busy with household chores, walking, and making quilts for her church's missionary program. The Maryland woman uses the neckties given her by friends and church members for quilt pieces. She has completed two large quilts which are being sold, the proceeds going to the overseas missionary program (of her church)."

To Mrs. Mary ...., 84, blind since 1941, the application of the expressions "old," "useless," or "handicapped" are inappropriate. Mrs. Mary is still energetically giving of herself and her talents.

This part of the chapter cannot be terminated without telling of a lady I once met. She was a great-grandmother many times over and was a spry little woman in her nineties. Her great-granddaughter introduced us principally because we were both interested in quilts. She had made quilts for her children and nieces, then for her grandchildren and grandnieces. At the time we met she was making quilts for a third generation. She said she still had thirty-three great grandnieces to make quilts for and that she would not be finished even then because four little girls of the fourth generation had arrived.

I wonder how many other lives might be saved from uselessness by the simple expedient of learning to piece quilt tops, or quilting lessons being added to the curriculum of craft classes in schools, day camps, correctional homes, hospitals, and adult educational programs.

Quilting used in hospitals is not a new idea. It was used in hospitals to help pass the time for patients recovering from wounds received during the Civil War. But when quilting lost favor with the rest of the country around the turn of the century, quilting in the hospitals was discontinued also. Certainly, if beauty is healing, and working with the hands aids recovery as many doctors tell us, then by the same token, quilting is healing.

"A thing of beauty is a joy forever." If that phrase describes anything it describes quilts. Any craft that is allowed to lie for years in disuse and sees the last craftsman die, is a lost art. Women here and there are keeping American quilting a living art. The purpose of this book is to interest our readers in this most American of all the crafts so that it may be passed along to our descendants as a living craft, reflecting not only this nation's past but revealing its present and foretelling its future as well.

INDEX OF QUILT NAMES

(See also general index which follows.)

189

INDEX

(See also index of quilt names.)